Gianni Ranaulo

Light Architecture
New Edge City

Preface by Antonino Saggio

Birkhäuser – Publishers for Architecture
Basel • Boston • Berlin

Translation from Italian into English: Stephen Jackson, Turin

A CIP catalogue record for this book is available from the Library of Congress, Washington D.C., USA.

Deutsche Bibliothek Cataloging-in-Publication Data

Ranaulo, Gianni:
Light architecture : new Edge city / Gianni Ranaulo. - Basel ; Boston ; Berlin : Birkhäuser, 2001
   ISBN 3-7643-6564-1

Original edition:
Light Architecture. New Edge City (Universale di Architettura 95, collana fondata da Bruno Zevi; La Rivoluzione Informatica, sezione a cura di Antonino Saggio).
© 2001 Testo & Immagine, Turin

© 2001 Birkhäuser – Publishers for Architecture, P.O. Box 133, CH-4010 Basel, Switzerland.
Member of the BertelsmannSpringer Publishing Group.
Printed on acid-free paper produced from chlorine-free pulp. TCF ∞
Printed in Italy
ISBN 3-7643-6564-1

9 8 7 6 5 4 3 2 1   http://www.birkhauser.ch

Contents

To Julie and Kama...

What harmony marks the rhythm of the world's spinning? We smile when it reaches the peak of its life, we tremble with terror when it returns to the dark. But the spin is always the same, it comes and goes, to the beat of an infinite music.

RABINDRĀNĀTH TAGORE

Leggere*

by Antonino Saggio

I thought a bit about the paragraph used as the introduction to this book. The quotes from *Lezioni Americane* are overused. In finding such an obvious quote, the scholar would make a face, the expert critic would smirk, the experienced reader shrug his shoulders. But many who will read *Light Architecture* will find that this quote, that recalls Perseus who held himself up by the winds, is very appropriate. Gianni Ranaulo absolutely could not have done better since this book makes the verb become adjective*. The architecture presented here by the author aspires to being light; the figures that accompany the text are light and like the reflections from a mirror. The pages turn as if blown by a breath and our light image. But do not be deceived, simplicity and lightness are difficult to obtain. Whether of the gymnast who spins in the air or a writer such as Italo Calvino, simplicity hides an essential and important substance.

I was led to working in architecture with the conviction that no limits must be placed on the design. As a consequence of this, there must be no misunderstanding between the materials and meanings, between the means and the ends. For a long time now, there has been an attempt to confine architecture to those hard materials of permanent structures: steel, reinforced concrete, stone and granite. As a consequence of this artificial confinement, terms have been invented that are reductive or simply ugly. When working with green spaces, trees, meadows, flowers or movements of earth or temporary structures, there was the "art of gardening"; when stone was substituted by papier-mâché, there was "set design"; when the materials were mobile, there was "furnishing"; when the objects were used in public spaces, there was "urban furnishing".

But if we turn the question around, everything becomes clear.

---

* The title, *Leggere*, has been left in Italian since I feel that the double meaning attributed to this term as it is used here in Italian cannot be duplicated in English. (Trans. Note: With the accent on different syllables in Italian, it can either mean the verb "to read" or the adjective "light".)

Design in relation to space is architecture but it is an architecture, depending on the case, needs and limitations, that uses different materials. From hard and permanent to light materials made of water, vegetation, reflections and light. This type of reasoning opens up a whole range of activities to the designer that, depending on the case and need, multiplies the possibilities of the project.

"Depending on the case and need" means, for example, that when the architect cannot build a wall of stone, he can build one with a spray of water; when he wants to redirect flows and lines, he can do it with a painting or projection (if we do not wish to use ancient obelisks); when he needs a new spatiality, he could perhaps use fabrics, curtains, or if he really needs them he can dig his spaces out of the earth or hang them in mid-air like a balloon.

Naturally, I knew that, in this expanded idea of design with a palette of light materials, the computer was a necessary tool in a thousand ways. But I could show very little in this direction beyond that great and brilliant forerunner Toyo Ito and something from the prophetic Jean Nouvel. The first merit of this book is in greatly expanding the number of examples and their operational and theoretical substrata, the second is in contributing to making concrete a new idea of the contemporary city.

Electronics and information technology systems can in fact furnish tools for the development of those "anti-zoning" areas around which modern life tends more and more to be arranged. Aside from being multi-functional zones (with activities that are productive, recreational, social and, in some cases, even residential) and helping in the needed return to nature in outlying areas frequently built with brutality and an insane density, they must, in order to actually function, have a nervous system made of technology, or rather information technology. This means systems of interactive control, of illumination, of "information" in the real sense. Only then will we have city sectors open to that multifunctionality and plurality of use that is the promise of the information technology civilization.

The problem as always is "how". For years Ranaulo has studied and applied precisely this idea to numerous designs. While going through the text you will also find many designs by artists, landscape artists and architects who move through this new territory heavily traveled by the light of information.

Miracles of Information Technology

Paul Virilio, and this quote is compulsory since this book gives concrete form to many of the French thinker's theories, spoke of the Electronic Gothic.

> Architecture is becoming a support for information, not to mention an advertising support and, in a broader sense, a mass media support [...] The Electronic Gothic of media buildings illuminates the crossroads – Times Square for example – in the same way that, in the Gothic cathedral, stained glass windows illuminated the nave or the presbytery to tell the story of the Church... time is no longer the time of a sequence alternating between day and night, but a time of immediacy, of instantaneousness and ubiquity; in other words, it possesses what in the past were the attributes of divinity.
> (From an interview by François Burkhardt published as an article in the first issue of *Crossing*).

Today, architecture and information technology go beyond the Electronic Gothic of the illuminating macro-object (the cathedral, much like a symbolic tower, in Bilbao of which I have spoken on other occasions) to once again directly face the issue of the urban setting. This happens not only because we have new tools for conceiving space (palimpsests, layers, dynamic diagrams, in-between spaces, emerging forms, etc.) but because the real and the virtual can now be combined in a manner once unheard of. As this book shows, this refers to the development of projection systems almost inside the shell itself of the building that give the effect of a sort of new, mass-media illusionism. So we can look forward to an Information Era Baroque, with its new Piazza Navonas, new Trevi Fountains and new Trinità dei Monti of 2006; in other words, a new, interactive urban choreography.

Ranaulo rightly tends to emphasize the technical aspect rather than the superficial scenic backdrop: the use of new types of glass that show rear projections but that during the day remain alive and transparent (and not drab, turned-off screens); the use of very thin marble that not only covers buildings but receives projected images at the same time; how to connect water or vegetation to computerized information networks, transforming them physically (nebulization for example, or vaporization or condensation, etc.); and how to contain information in these new ethereal supports. In other words, a job that is also difficult, with technical engineering that reminds us of the work behind the facades of Versailles or Caserta, a lot of subterranean construction (building dams, digging canals, pumping systems, etc.) without which nothing would have seen the light.

In summary, this book, with its illustrative material, highlights three aspects worth remembering; aspects the reader quickly notices.

1. No qualitative difference exists in the methods used by architecture. Instead of doing a very costly renewal of an old urban landmark, such as a skyscraper, sprays of nebulized water can be set up around it on which images are projected. This revives the area, can be performed at very low cost and opens a new informational space for everyone since both the revolt of the poor as well as the success of the rich can be projected on those rings.

2. There is no longer any difference between first level communication (the architecture itself that is transformed into an object of information) and second level communication (i.e. information technology systems that rely on screens that are "added" to the building). The building as a whole becomes a communicative vector and architectural object at the same time.

3. Finally, no difference exists between design in the city center or outlying areas. The information and projection systems presented in this book indicate practical solutions that regard just as much those "black holes" in abandoned urban areas as they do those nerve centers of old cities or even archeological sites.

In short, "No design limits" means that, thanks to electronics, we can help open up the city to the complex intellectual and technical procedure called architectural design that makes up a significant framework in present day reality. And our awareness of reality, that now may have several components considered in the past as belonging to divinity (as mentioned in that enlightened observation quoted earlier) is seen in our, still astonished, gazes.

www.arc.uniroma1.it/Saggio/

1. The Origins

> In certain moments, it seemed to me as if the world were turning completely to stone: a slow petrification more or less advanced depending on the people and places, but one that did not spare any aspect of life. It was as if no one could escape the relentless gaze of the Medusa. The only hero capable of cutting off the head of the Medusa was Perseus who flew on winged sandals, Perseus who did not turn his gaze on the face of the Gorgon but only her image reflected in the bronze shield. […] To cut off the head of Medusa without letting himself be petrified, Perseus held himself up on the lightest support, the winds and clouds, and turned his gaze on that which could only be revealed in an indirect vision, an image captured by a mirror. (Calvino 88)

"It seemed to me as if the world were turning completely to stone": in this slow petrification spoken of by Italo Calvino in his celebrated reflections on writing, we can recognize the signs of the crisis experienced by the world of architecture. For some time now, we have been effectively witnessing a slow petrification of architecture, that becomes heavier and heavier, more and more static, and continually older, as if we were unable to detach ourselves from that original idea of immortality that has always obsessed us, the desire to make ourselves immortal through stone.

The truth is that the world has changed and with it our societies, cultures and the cities where we live, architecture must move in the direction of the world and be employed in the service of mankind. The immortality of architecture, the holiness of the architectural site, no longer have any reason to exist. This concept has been overcome. Architecture must move as fast as the world in which we live and must give experiences that are just as fast, since our passage through the world is fast.

There are few truly innovative ideas in the field of architecture: the absence is felt of a reversal of trends that would give a general view of the phenomena in present society. The architect must be like a blade that cuts society into its various aspects (cinema, fashion, advertising, culture); he must follow the progress of the world and invent new forms of projects. The evolution of the world, of cities and their systems (continually faster and more complex) implies a consequent evolution in the field of architecture as well. Consider the great flows – both human and mechanical – of circulation, the *pôles d'échange* where most people today arrive, stop, wait, meet and then depart again. These have substituted traditional gathering places: town squares, bars. This phenomena requires a dynamic architecture that provides the functions necessary for managing these flows; an architecture that brings together a series of practical and entertaining services along with information (consider the metro station of Chatelet-les Halles in Paris, with its boutiques, cinemas, bars and so forth: a utopia made real during the 1960s; today, a reality we need).

Among the various trends that developed beginning in the 1980s, transparency is the one that takes on the greatest importance, especially because of the lack of any real idea in those years, of any leading school of thought capable of creating a reversal of trends with respect to the past. Transparency was therefore the only possibility for architecture to express a concept of innovation. Many positive results were achieved by some architects (though

Les Halles, Paris.

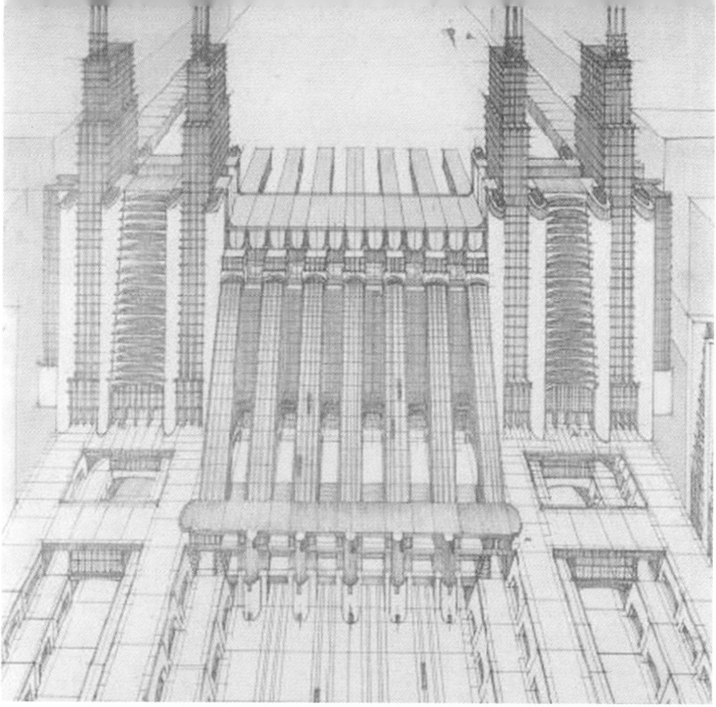

Above: Antonio Sant'Elia, Stazione d'aeroplani e treni ferroviari, 1914. Below: Paul Andreu, Jean Marie Duthilleul, Etienne Tricaud, TGV station, Charles de Gaulle Airport, Roissy, Paris, 1994.

powerfully inspired by the play of transparencies of Mies van der Rohe), first and foremost among them Jean Nouvel, who promoted, with the help of philosophers such as Jean Baudrillard and Paul Virilio, a clear, coherent debate on the phenomena of contemporary society.

There are however many cases where transparency generated a high-tech architecture, made of cables and wires, tubes and conduits, almost as if to assign problems of an architectural nature to technology. In reality, with no real idea, all reference parameters are lost: the shell becomes empty and meaningless; spatial hierarchies disappear; the relationship between form and function is annulled; the parameter of the *genius loci*, of the specific nature of a building changes completely.

A situation of great ambiguity is created so that everything appears equal: lacking any authentic relationship between form and function, every school is the same and a court house is the same as a museum that is the same as a media library; since there is no close relationship to the place, any place is fine; you can move your project from one space to another and from one city to another. A contextualization of the site no longer exists, we find ourselves facing a dictatorship of transparency in which, seduced by high-tech systems, the facade, the skin, becomes much more important than the container itself. The consequence is a great cultural void, a great emptiness of ideas that has led to a vast production of products of obvious mediocrity, masked behind a high-tech, pseudo-quality.

Therefore, a further shift was verified away from the pressing problems of current society, away from considerations of the conditions of mankind in the modern urban environment, and finally away from the problems of the city itself. So attempts were made at resolving these problems, attempts with subsequent, inevitable failures; such as when, instead of evaluating the issues related to a project in an outlying area, a high school is built, sustaining very high costs, with sophisticated structures and windows; inevitably, the building becomes the object of contention, even vandalism; it becomes the target of social aggression produced by urban deprivation. Here, sophisticated architecture is imposed on a neighborhood where there are many much greater problems to be faced. (This is also the result of a political administration that in order to gain the sympathies of public opinion, avails itself of the most

well known architects without reflecting on the real necessities of managing spaces.) Or like those, later failed, attempts from the 1960s: for example the architecture of the satellite cities, the garden cities, based of the model of Le Corbusier's *Ville Radieuse*; all choices that led to the contemporary problems of urban violence and estrangement.
Now we know that was not the solution and the escape from the cities has been transformed into a return to the cities. At the same time, we need nature and leave for the countryside on the

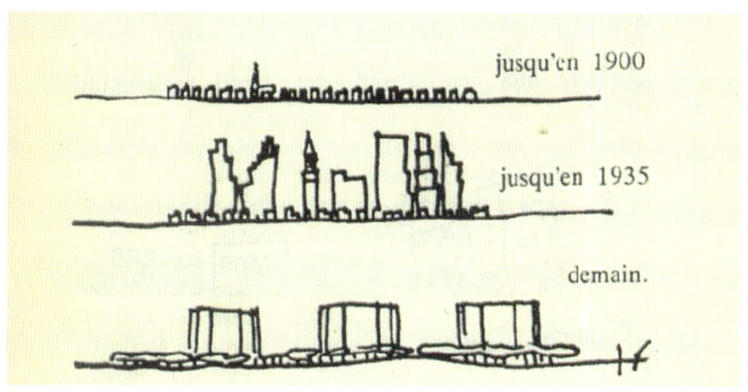

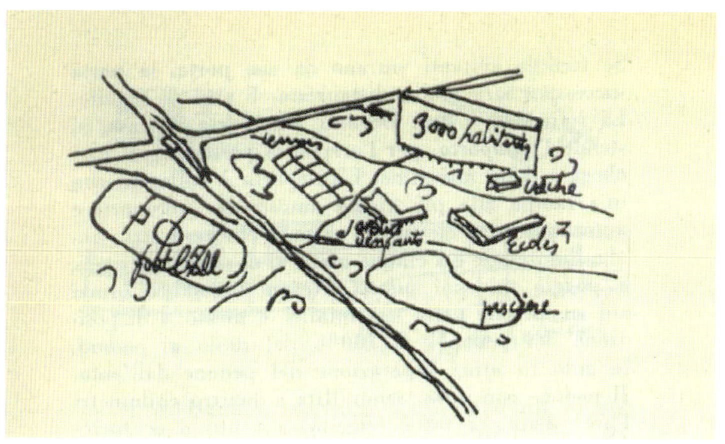

Le Corbusier, Sketches on the growth of New York, 1935.

weekends. But we also need technology and bring along our mobile phones, portable computers, televisions, etc. We live in a world where, on the one hand, technologies have taken the upper hand and, on the other, a great need has arisen for a return to the natural state. In reality, we almost no longer move any more, we live in a state of constant immobility because of the great flow of information that arrives to us comfortably on our computer; information that arrives too quickly, information that, thanks to the Internet, has noticeably reduced distances (with various problems, among them Internet dependency, i.e. IRP or Internet Related Pathology, that according to the Association of American Psychologists strikes around 10% of all net users). The Internet, the revolution of the third millennium, with its potentials and dangers, its positive and innovative, as well as destructive, aspects (Paul Virilio speaks of an "information bomb"), is a phenomenon that has not only changed our way of living, but has destroyed all preceding reference parameters: the stock exchange, economy, political power.

Architecture can not ignore these changes. It must make progress its own; must exploit it to its own advantage (since the true utopia

Doug Aitken, Electric Earth, *1999.*

of the third millennium is the fusion between chaos and nature), creating, like the "New Economy", a "New Architecture" that would go beyond the parameters of "constructed" architecture in order to move onto the plane of the "non-constructed", the "non visible".

Fritz Lang, Metropolis, *1927.*

In order to understand more clearly how the idea of a new form of architecture was born, three elements must be kept in mind that changed the image of contemporary architecture: the automobile, electricity and advertising. The automobile, changing the perception of the static and dynamic, changed the image of architecture from two-dimensional to three-dimensional and transformed it into a rapid architecture in movement. Electricity changed the genetic code of architecture, not only as regards the control of the climate of the environment but above all because of illumination that changed architecture from dark to luminous, lengthening the period of life in the cities where now we live twenty-four hours a day, with different flows and targets in the passage from day to night. Advertising has further changed the image of architecture and the city. Consider Times Square even twenty years ago, or Piccadilly Circus, where the chaos of images now reigns supreme: information, billboards, all types of signs, a visual bombardment

Sarah Morris, Midtown Series, *1999.*

Times Square, New York.

that older cities built around historic centers could never risk. Even though Times Square is the icon of the modern city, at the same time that image is not part of our collective imagination.

These three aspects have great importance from the point of view of architectural culture and are part of the new vision of an architecture that is first of all dynamic and in movement like the automobile; in the second place, an architecture that, like the city (transformed from day to night by its lights, by day sober and elegant, by night seductive, magic and playful) is mimetically integrated into the urban space; in the third place, one that gives order to the chaos of information, creating significant points of reference.

The idea is precisely that of evolution, so that architecture, utilizing modern scientific technologies, becomes an alternative solution to urban problems, acting upon contemporary reality no longer simply on the level of construction. An architecture that modifies and revives the city, building rapidly (times today are rapid, planning must be done at the speed of light, we must have an idea, create it and immediately apply it), intelligently (create different design possibilities, lighter, even temporary, that are integrated into the urban space as "micro-renewals" of spaces) and with the contribution of young people (because the ability of being modern and expressing a creative force that allows a project to have its own reason for existing in a determined place belongs specifically to the young: we should not wait for ideas to get old, as happens frequently, out of a lack of structures that support the work of

young, talented architects); a new architecture that is also taken less seriously; the idea must be overcome of architecture as something heavy, with long, slow delivery times or projects that last for years. Instead projects must be conceived, even in a detached manner, that at times are not real architecture but artistic creations that transfigure a space; an architecture that may also be temporary, with a limited life time, but perfectly positioned in the time in which it was created. And today's technological means allow us to affect these changes.

Left: Gianni Ranaulo, Fin Foxile, *2000. Right: Lotek, Vertical Leisure Center, New York.*

2. The Idea

The image can no longer imagine the real because it is itself the real, it can not longer transcend it, transfigure it, dream it, because it is the virtual reality. In the virtual reality, it is as if things had swallowed their own mirror. And having swallowed their own mirror, had become transparent to themselves […] and the things, entirely known to themselves in their visibility, in their virtuality are now only written on a screen […]. Today, all things want to manifest themselves […] the subject is no longer at the origin of the process but is only the agent of the objective irony of the world. It is no longer the subject that represents the world (I will be your mirror!), it is the object that shatters the subject and subtly, through all our technologies, imposes on it its presence and its aleatoric form. […] At the confines of hyper-visibility, of virtuality, is there still a place for an image, for an authentic strategy of forms and appearances? […] We would need illusionists who understand that all art is first a trompe-l'oeil, a deception of sight and deception of life […] So as to rediscover, through the illusion, a form of fundamental seduction. (Baudrillard 97)

Light Architecture® is an attempt at a synthesis between two worlds still considered incompatible: the real world and the virtual world. The need for this fusion has now become obvious; a fusion that has entered into our imagery. We have several early examples of this fusion, especially in the field of television.
(An interesting example, one that helps us understand how reference parameters have changed in the world of infant imagination, is the BBC television program with the animated *Teletubbies* puppets, now shown in other countries. Utilizing puppets with a screen on their bellies where images are projected that, from time to time, depending on the teaching needs, show different aspects of daily life, the program manages to create a fusion between the virtual world and the real one by presenting elements from both one and the other – real meadows and fake skies, real objects and fake people, etc. – aiming at transmitting traditional values through the use of a modern medium.)
Light Architecture proposes unifying virtual space with concrete reality in order to maintain a unity of perception of the real and thus create a single dimension: "stereoreality", where everything is the result of those two spaces. In particular, to fight the risk of

Teletubbies, *launched by the BBC, 1995.*   *Shigeko Kubota*, Sexual Healing, *2000.*

isolation by the computer and dependency on the Internet created by the relationship with virtual reality, we are working on integration on an urban scale, i.e. a new dimension of architecture
inside the city. Since the real creation of the global village happens
in the city, a shift must be made from the individual sphere and
private sphere (computer, television, etc.) to the collective sphere
of the urban scene, from the global village to the "glocal village".
Just as architects from the Renaissance created perspective as a
new relationship with reality, a mathematical reconstruction of
reality through geometry, so today the architect must create a
new relationship with reality using a stereoscopic perspective, i.e.
a perspective that is at the same time one of real space and one
of virtual time-space, of the "live", real time that allows communication and interaction with the world precisely in the moment
when the action takes place. The city of the future in fact foresees
the co-existence of two urban realities: the real city (with its center, its periphery and the well-known problems that presently
characterize it) and the virtual city, that exercises an enormous
influence on the former, that has several examples already especially in the realm of television.
The integration between real and virtual on the city level is creat-

ed by utilizing every new technology available, including experimental techniques used in films for special effects, in order to obtain applications that create highly spectacular architectural projects (that in some way will soften the impact on the public and citizens) and contain an important element of interaction with the citizens themselves.

A relationship of osmosis almost exists between new architectural trends and the inhabitant of the modern city. Each project is alive to the extent that the city and its inhabitants allow it to exist. We are therefore witnessing an important change in the function of the citizen, from passive spectator to active, interactive actor, i.e. an "interactor", capable of entering the urban context and interacting with it. In reuniting the real and virtual in one single world and making the citizen an active part of the structure, interactivity becomes the vital energy of the new system, opposing not only the canons of traditional architecture, presented as a dominant element in its contact with mankind, but also those same television networks where the virtual space becomes much more important than the real physical space. (Consider the dangers of several recent television programs that, beginning with the success of the webcam phenomenon on the Internet, take voyeurism to extremes, putting people in a condition of leaving the real space in which they live in order to transfer themselves into a virtual space. A celebrated example is the success met by the television program *Big Brother* in which the participants activate a sort of self-hibernation of their ego, for a certain period freezing their personality, their life, their social contribution.)

The complete and concrete activation of these plans is confirmed in the Media Building, in which it is Light Architecture, applied to a single building, that creates a real image of fusion between the two worlds, in which the spectacularization of physical flows is fused with the spectacularization of virtual flows in a single glass medium. The interface with the citizen, the possibility given him to interact with his urban context, is important because it represents a step forward in the desire to democratize the process of appropriating public space, one that began with "tags", graffiti on city walls. Light Architecture – applied in particular to the Media Building – allows people to interact on the visual level, appropriating freely, and at no cost, a public space (and therefore not merely a space on the virtual level, as happens on the Internet). We would like this to be a starting point for a process of democratization on a global scale, including one against the monopoly of the great advertising brands that now bombard the citizen from every corner of the city.

The Media Building – still considered a utopia during the 1960s, subsequently designed by avant-garde architects and now actually constructed in metropolises like New York, Shanghai and Las Vegas – is thus the concrete realization on an urban scale of the fusion of the real world and virtual world, the transfer from the information network universe of the private and individual sphere, from the single computer work station to the collective scale of public space. In an era of pure information, such as the one we are presently experiencing, the Media Building, through the use of interactive multimedia facades, is introduced as a new architectural structure in which the function of information prevails over that of habitation.

Paul Virilio speaks quite a bit about the importance of information

Gianni Ranaulo, Media Building Piazza Garibaldi, *Naples, 2000.*

in modern architecture, starting from the concept that, in physics, matter is made up of three dimensions: mass, energy and information.

> From the beginning architects have shaped mass, just as they have utilized energy; information on the other hand has still not been really used. If we consider a cathedral, this constitutes a means of mass communication. During the Middle Ages, information was transmitted through its stained glass windows, sculptures, tapestries, mosaics […]. But this information was fixed, static, constant, only renewed through the action of language and songs. Today, on the other hand, we are entering an age when information is active and interactive; in other words, we are no longer just dealing with frescoes on walls, sculptures in niches or stained glass windows, but with a place of action and interaction. Because of this, the architect must apply himself to this third dimension […] The "media building" is a building that preferably houses information rather than habitation, no matter what the type. (Virilio 98)

Light Architecture, through the Media Building, proposes to give architecture back its fundamental role as an information vector, aiming towards an architecture that informs and communicates. In a society where the image acquires continually more importance because of its immediate effectiveness on the citizen – which gives rise to a constant search for continually more seductive and persuasive images – architectural surfaces are transformed into supports for communication that go beyond the traditional canons of architecture, almost to the point of turning images themselves into construction materials.

The Media Building is, in effect, a tool of communication and interaction; it is the place where, through interactive multimedia facades, information is communicated and exchanged on an urban level: institutional and cultural information, progressive advertising, Internet, trailers, SMSs, etc. The use of advertising as a source of information allows notable reductions in costs and production times. (Just consider that every day in Italy, posters and billboards reach 14.1 million people and reach another 14.4 many times over the course of a week. Furthermore, a survey conducted during November 1997 showed a very high use of poster and billboard advertising, affecting 61% of the populace.) Advertising is a form of self-financing for the building, a potential rebuilding element since the profits from advertising information are high enough to guarantee the profitability of a building, with the result of faster projects at lower cost.

With the Media Building, in addition to the traditional lights of the city that surround us every day, there are new lights, screens in movement, trans-apparent surfaces that transform urban architecture into a daily *événément* in constant change and evolution.

Another important aspect of Light Architecture is the possibility of acting on the city, modifying it and renewing it, through "micro-interventions of urban surgery".

Without employing great urban design studies, and therefore with the possibility of acting rapidly on an area with a short term project, Light Architecture can be used to carry out small electroshocks for reviving sleeping areas of cities: outlying areas, small centers, areas in search of an identity because of the lack of a historic fabric, historic centers devastated by the architecture of speculation (for example in Italy with its problems created by building speculators and engineers in the 1960s), areas that should be demolished and rebuilt (as in America where the economic dynamo is strong enough to allow the demolition and rapid reconstruction of entire areas thanks to the self-regeneration of capital).

In Europe, and particularly in Italy, modern architecture has produced very little and what remains is the devastating architecture of the 1960s. There being no system at present like the American one, Light Architecture is seen as a rapid and effective remedy for carrying out the "make-over" projects that cities need.

If we consider the history of dwellings, from caves to lake dwelling platforms up until the houses of today, we realize that the problems and necessities of the past have not substantially changed. Just as caves were inhabited out of man's necessity to defend himself from nature, so today too we close ourselves up in our dwellings in order to defend ourselves from both nature and man himself. The inhabited cell has always been the most important space for man, who over the course of time has constantly attempted to make it perfect but in reality has never managed to improve and renew the quality of habitation; as Heidegger said:

Rampe Sant'Antonio, Naples.

GIANNI RANAULO, *CITY WEB*, NAPLES, 1998

This project is an example of the renewal of "black holes in the city", the result of building speculation during the 1950s. The existing structure, in reinforced concrete, supporting the piazza, situated on one of the most scenic spots in Naples, has never had any intended use. The idea is to exploit the existing skeleton to create not only a "Piazza Telematica" ["Information Technology Square"], but also a large, interactive multi-media center; this way the site is renewed and given a new image, while at the same time creating a point of interest for tourists that could reactivate the entire neighborhood (the urban axis that connects the piazza to Mergellina Station). The projects includes the construction of balconies and glass ramps, a double skin of "trans-apparent" glass (that gives a view of the internal structure) and a roof of photovoltaic glass (so that the energy requirements for the entire structure derive from solar energy). Each cell of the building, furnished with a webcam, is virtually reconstructed depending on the required environment and becomes a multimedia space to be used as a work place.

Gianni Ranaulo, City Web, Naples, 1998.

Gianni Ranaulo, Black Stone, *Alicudi, 1995.*

"Build, inhabit, think". If information is becoming more and more important, if we utilize the information vector as the soul of the new quality of habitation, then we must also stop and think, in order to design in a way that is different and more in line with today's real needs.

Light Architecture, in all its different expressions, could be a key element in changing and improving the parameters of habitation: it allows us to design with different, lighter tools (sprays of water, carbon fiber, photovoltaic glass, composite materials, inflatable materials, etc.) with the possibility of new forms of projects.

Gianni Ranaulo, Swelling Screen, *1995.*

Olafur Eliasson, Thoka, *1995.*

Light Architecture

KEY WORDS / CONCEPTS

1) *"Glocal" Village*: from the individual sphere of the private screen to the collective sphere of the urban scene, from the Local Village to the Global Village.
2) *Stereoreality*: integration of the virtual world and the real world into one single reality.
3) *The Global Screen*: new Internet scenario.
4) *Interactor*: from passive spectators, citizens become active, interactive actors.
5) *Metamorphose*: an architecture that is integrated into the urban space in a mimetic way so that the life of the city changes from day to night.
6) *Media Building*: buildings are transformed into vectors of information and communication.
7) *Immaterial Architecture*: use of immaterial elements such as water and light.
8) *Free-thought*: thinking, designing and building in short times.
9) *B2B*: the self-financing of architecture, thanks to new financial flows – New Economy, Mass Media, New Technology.

PROJECT METHODS

1) Restoration of existing buildings.
2) Animation of natural elements within the landscape.
3) Virtual restoration of archeological and historic sites.
4) Recovery of outlying urban areas and *terrains vagues*.
5) Contextual/ecological micro-projects to stop the pollution of transport and circulation axes.
6) Artistic projects – not necessarily true architecture – to transfigure a space, even if temporarily.
7) Projects of urban micro-surgery (*archi-maquillage*).
8) "Piazze telematiche" ["Information Technology Town Squares"]: recovery of the function of meeting in the town square thanks to interactive multimedia systems.
9) Spectacularization of monuments.

Above: Erick Van Egeraat Associated, ING Bank, Budapest, 1998?; Below: Gianni Ranaulo, Maison di Retraite de Rabais, 1994-98. The building has a self-illuminating facade that integrates natural and artificial light; with insufficient daylight, the receiving cells activate the system of self-illumination located in the glass brise-soleil; from the inside, the impression is one of constant light even on the grayest days of the year.

Regarding this subject, it is interesting to note how the term "light" has taken on more and more importance over the last few years in different commercial sectors, almost coinciding with the new trends in the architecture of transparency. We find different "light" products on the market, indicating the positive effect of the term itself on the client. A well-known example is Coke Light; one that has met with decidedly greater success than Diet Coke, same product, different name. And hence an entire series of products that utilize the term "light" or recall it in their appearance; in cosmetics, a whole line of "light" products has been introduced, expressing both transparency and purity, cosmetics without scents or colors. What counts is the product reduced to its essence; packaging and advertising become the skin, infused with all the characteristics that the

product lacks. Architecture – that, as we have already said, must reflect society in its different aspects – follows this line of development: the content is reduced to the essential, to its primary function; the container assumes a new importance and transmits the necessary information.

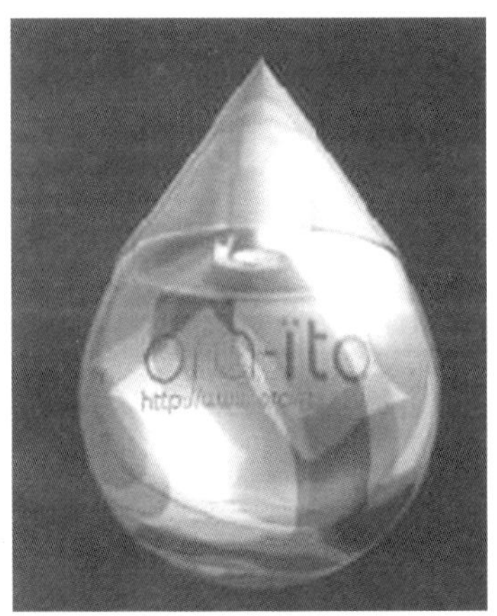

LE FEU D'ISSEY LIGHT

In Light Architecture the process becomes even more evident: the relationship between form and function is established not only in the quality of the form, but above all in the skin, in the container that through a sequence of transparent textures defines the internal product of the architectural object.

In this phase of modifying reality, Light Architecture, introduced as a new architectural trend that plays on the use of "light" – both in the sense of illumination, lightweight materials and the architecture's ironic view of itself, more detached, even temporary – and activating a fusion of the real and the virtual on the urban scene as one of the possible configurations of contemporary society, could be seen as a solution to the problems of today's cities and an ideological foundation for the construction of the city of the future.

Gianni Ranaulo, Musée de l'imaginaire, *Paris, 1999.*

3. The Projects

> If I wanted to choose an auspicious symbol for facing the new millennium, I would choose this one: the agile, improvised leap of the poet-philosopher who rises up on the heaviness of the world, showing that its gravity contains the secret of lightness [...]. In his poetry [Cavalcanti], the "dramatis personae" are more than human characters; they are luminous rays, optical images, and most of all those immaterial impulses or messages he calls "spirits". [...] In other words, we are always dealing with something distinguished by three characteristics: 1) it is very light; 2) it is in movement; 3) it is a vector of information. (Calvino 86)

In this third section, the elements and characteristics that distinguish Light Architecture become completely realized in the designs, constructions and projects you will find listed, supported by a brief description and related images. In line with a research parameter of light applications, the examples have been divided into the three categories listed by Calvino – lightness, movement, information – subdivided in turn into other categories. This is a strictly conceptual division; in fact, a connecting thread does exist in that each project taken under consideration contains all the characteristics belonging to Light Architecture: it is light; contains an element of movement; and is a vector of information.

The division we apply here, based on the consideration of the predominant aspects of a project, helps in some way to comprehend the application of the characteristics and contents of Light Architecture theorized up till now. Many artists and architects, in one way or another, have influenced the birth of this theory; many works reflect this theory and have several characteristics belonging to Light Architecture. We have chosen several examples, the most important, that have left a mark on architecture over the last few years.

3.1 Lightness

Several projects are included in this category that utilize Light Architecture under the definition of lightness: lightness as a concept, lightness of image, lightness as a temporary element, lightness as transparency, lightness as a loss of gravity, etc. In all these cases, we continually see a transparency that is not obvious, not evident, facades that give a view inside without uncovering everything since, as the literary critic Jean Starobinski said in his essay *Poppaea's Veil* (1989), "the hidden fascinates".

Above: Asymptote, Aarhus Univers Theatre, Denmark, 1996. Below: Santiago Calatrava, Alamillo Bridge, Seville, 1987-1992.

Above: Sigheru Ban, Odawara Pavilion. Completed in April 1990 after just three and a half months of work. The walls are composed of 350 cardboard tubes, each 8 meters long and 53 centimeters in diameter. Below: John M. Johansen, Air Quilt System. This is an example of a pneumatic command of space. This mechanism was developed to produce closed spaces capable of changing size and shape. The double plastic skin is modified, becoming concave instead of convex, by shifting compressed air from one room to the another. This manipulation of space allows new experiences in architecture.

3.1.1 CONCEPTUAL LIGHTNESS

The search for lightness can be concentrated in a single concept: the challenge of mass, of the weight of architecture, the problem of gravity. The problem of the architectural mass that gravitates toward the ground and leads to the earth – a fundamental theme that has inspired different architects and artists over the years – is resolved with the use of lighter architecture, thin pillars, empty spaces as load bearing structures, the vertical dimension. The result is a series of light, evanescent and poetic constructions that in their essence recall the natural elements: air, water, light.

Dennis Oppenheim, Stage Set for a Film, *1999.*

Toyo Ito, Mediatheque, Sendai, 1997

This project starts by abandoning the archetypal idea of an art museum or a library to give rise to a new form and new idea of architecture: the "mediatheque". Three principal elements characterize this building: the flat plates; the light latticework pillars similar to trees that vertically penetrate the plates, organizing them and integrating themselves into them; the skin of the building not only separates the inside from the outside but surrounds the spaces at the base and top of the structure and is seen as a double glass skin that shapes the facade on the main road. The latticework pillars are important in that they are flexible, structural components that act as a line of vertical traffic and a space in which the various types of energy – light, air, water, sound, etc. – and information flow. With these three simple elements, the Mediatheque is a place of integration between a primitive space, closely connected to nature (air, water, light) and a virtual space connected to the world through a network of electrons that represent human activities.

Jean Nouvel, *Tour Sans Fins*, Paris, 1989

This project explores the problem of verticality and the limits of a building through a double "disappearance": one at the base of the building, so that it seems to rise up from a crater, and a disappearance at the top of the tower. In effect, the facade gradually dematerializes, continually more light and evanescent, a tenuous air-structure that dissolves into the sky. The evanescence of the tower is also underlined by colored glass sections that mark the different altitudes; at night, the effect is accentuated by colored lights. 420 meters high, with a diameter of 143 meters at the base, the tower presents itself as a simple, immaterial construction, the expression of a conceptually infinite vertical tension.

On 22 September 1985, a group of three hundred workers completed this project by Christo & Jeanne-Claude which utilized 40,876 square meters of canvas to cover the vaults of the twelve arches of the bridge, 13,076 meters of rope to secure the canvas and more than 12 metric tonnes of steel chain fastened to the base of each pillar. On its completion, all the details of the bridge's construction became invisible, as if, wrote Werner Spies, "it had been designed by Adolf Loos, for whom any ornament is a crime". The final visual impression was that of a modern, aerodynamic architecture that nevertheless preserved a few curiously Medieval character-istics.

GIANNI RANAULO AND HUGH DUTTON, ASI, ROME, 2000

This project – presented at the international competition held by the ASI – starts from the idea of the loss of gravity and the condition of astronauts in space, as a metaphor for a place suspended between the earth and sky. The architecture of the building is therefore light and dynamic at the same time: a square spiral that progresses along itself to metaphorically run at times toward the sky, at times toward the earth. The skyline of the project in cross-section also recalls that of the ASI satellites sent into orbit. A large, interactive, multimedia facade receives images and information from space in real time; the intention here is not only educational but also poetic: like a mirror of consciousness, the images of space fascinate and frighten at the same time, bringing the spectator back to the reality in which he lives, so small seen from space that it gives a new point of view on life and its problems.

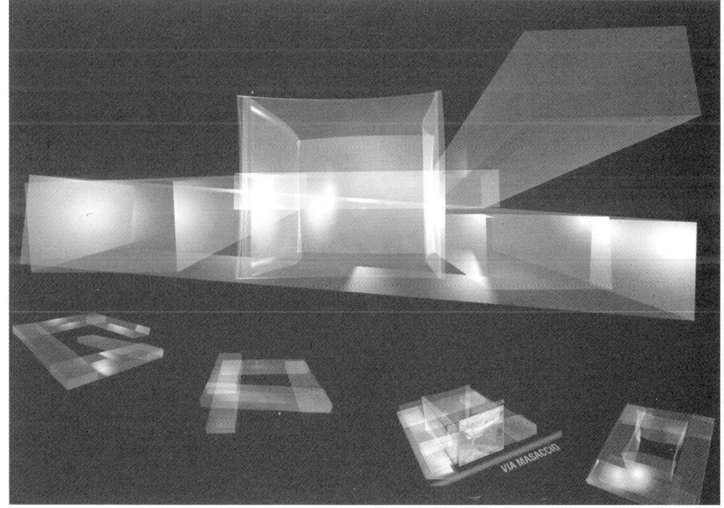

Aldo Rossi, Il Teatro del mondo, *1989.*

Fishermen's Shed in Gironde.

Hunter's Shack.

G. Ranaulo, Tana Mesu, *Anakao, Mada-gascar, 2000.*

J. Nouvel, Truck Design, *1990.*

3.1.2 CONSTRUCTIVE LIGHTNESS

Projects and works are represented in this category that apply Light Architecture in its most obvious aspect of light and lightness. However, it is important to underline that applications also come under this category that have their own reason for existing since they themselves are light.

Beginning with the exhibit *Light Construction*, presented by MoMA in New York in 1996, where a series of constructions were presented that were closely connected to the concept of transparency, light and lightness, we would like to also bring together in this category all those existing constructions that have a light impact on the city or territory – such as sheds, platforms, spontaneous rural constructions, etc. – and the temporary types of architecture that transfigure the image of the city – installations for work site logistics, restorations, sheet metal and the large wooden panels that until a few years ago were utilized in place of the pictorial canvases that today substitute them in every corner of the city. Consider the restoration of the church of Saint-Augustin in Paris: an extraordinary structure of sheet metal and wood that in some way recalled the *Teatro del Mondo* by Aldo Rossi presented at the Venice "Biennale". These are light, temporary projects that change the image of existing architecture, almost hypermodern constructions that are superimposed on fixed, heavy structures and in certain cases allow the city to expand by implosion, chance elements that transfigure a space and renew the city.

Coop Himmelb(l)au, Power and Freedom – Non Verbal Communication, 2000.

Jean Nouvel, Fondation Cartier, Paris, 1994

The site where the headquarters of the Cartier Foundation now stands in the historic center of Paris was previously occupied by a nineteenth century villa surrounded by an expansive garden with many trees, among them a giant cedar of Lebanon planted by Chateaubriand, one of the most illustrious occupants of the villa. In constructing the new building, Nouvel had to stay within the area previously occupied by the villa, leaving the green space intact. The appeal of the Cartier Foundation lies in Nouvel's ability to not only develop a vertical structure but also and above all to neutralize and exploit the imposed limits, utilizing a glass skin that gives an interior view both of the inner structure as well as the rear garden. Using three parallel glass surfaces, Nouvel creates an ambiguity so that visitors do not know if what they see is a real image or a reflection, everything immersed in a game of light and shadow that intentionally goes beyond transparency in order to evoke an expressive response.

DAN GRAHAM, *TWO-WAY MIRROR CYLINDER INSIDE CUBE*, NEW YORK, 1981-1991

Dan Graham, a conceptual artist whose sculptures and installations exist at the confines between art and architecture, uses the materials of modernist architecture to emphasize the relationships and differences between the inside and outside, between private and public spaces, placing at the center of his work the processes of seeing and being seen. The transparent surfaces in fact permit not only seeing but also being seen by one another; the reflecting surfaces react to the natural world, changing in relation to the light and the movement of the sun and clouds. In this installation, created for the roof of the DIA Center for the Arts in New York, the artist creates an urban park on a reduced scale to spark a reconsideration of the urban environment and the idea of neutral space.

Gianni Ranaulo, *Wheat-loft*, Capalbio, 2001

The design for Wheat-loft in Capalbio, in the Maremma marshes of Tuscany, calls for the creation of a dwelling in harmony with nature and the surrounding environment, capable of keeping the memory of the place alive. The load bearing structure of the house is in fact the hay loft itself, re-interpreted in a modern vein. The entire structure of the dwelling –a maison domotique where the energy network is run by computer – is in steel and assembled without bolts; the horizontal plateaux on different levels follow the lay of the land; the roof, of photovoltaic panels, ensures autonomous energy. The enclosure in glass gives a continuity between the inside and outside and the only full volumes visible (in composite material) see the constant presence of the hay itself.

Cross-section of the project.

The hay loft before the project.

GIANNI RANAULO, *NIGHT & DAY*, ALCAMO, 1992-94

This creation attempts to represent the duality between day and night, good and evil. The section that symbolizes night is contained in a cube of black, unfinished cement; the section that symbolizes day is represented by a veil of entirely transparent glass, with a steel structure, that houses a large golden stone: the living room, closed off from the street side and open to the landscape. The materials in the daytime section are aluminum, perforated sheet metal and glass, that give reality to the concepts of lightness, clarity and transparency. In the nighttime section, the black block of cement closes off the interior space. The black cube and golden stone recall the Arab-Norman influence on local architecture. The architecture adapts itself to the morphology of the site, following the curve of the road and reinforcing the spectacular view of the Gulf of Palermo.

KOVAC MALONE, IKON TOWER, LITTLE LATROBE STREET, MELBOURNE, 2000

Built out of steel, cement and carbon fiber, this building is connected to a fiber optic network that feeds information to the central computer system. The building houses services, private apartments and offices and is designed to communicate with its occupants. The exterior is a translucent, fluid mass, equipped with high technology sensors that record variations in the weather in order to regulate the interior temperature. Radio signals substitute cables for illumination and the roof acts as an energy generator for all the electrical operations of the building.

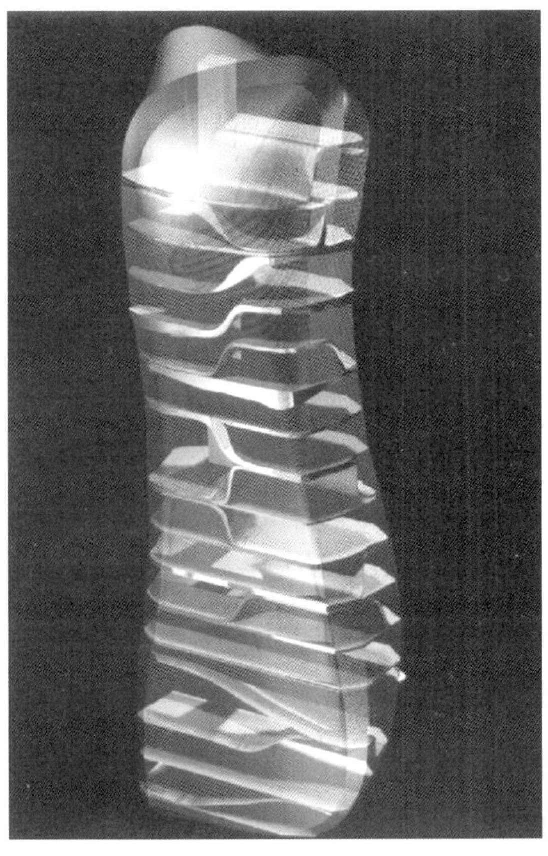

3.1.3 IMMATERIAL LIGHTNESS

In this section, projects and constructions are presented that utilize immaterial elements, such as water and light, to shape a space. Beginning with the use of glass as transparency, the next step is to conceptualize the disappearance of the glass into the water that composes it (glass has the same molecular composition as water). In the following projects, water has an important function as an immaterial support that hides the load bearing structure or as a screen that defines the space or even as an ecological element that revives the environment. Light has for some time been used in cities, frequently as an element of spectacularization. The *mise en lumière* of monuments is a theme frequently considered and resolved by great artists, though just as frequently poorly resolved by companies employed in illuminating our cities with no attention given to monuments with the result that they end up making them look ridiculous. In reality, an attentive and sophisticated use of light can give extraordinary results and revitalize not only monuments or single buildings but also blighted areas of the city.

Gianni Ranaulo, Piazze Telematiche, Naples, 1998. The covering of the facade (that hides the stairways and emergency exits) is a double skin composed of a glass fiber network over which water flows: at night, a support for the projection of images: by day, an ecological element for creating a micro-climate that renews and regenerates the surrounding environment.

Yann Kersalé, Irreversible Light, Grand Palais, Paris, 1987.

Jean Nouvel, Opera de Lyon, illumination by Yann Kersalé, Lyon, 1993.

Illumination of the Eiffel Tower, Societé Nouvelle Tour Eiffel, 2000.

Norman Foster, Reichstag, Berlin, 2000.

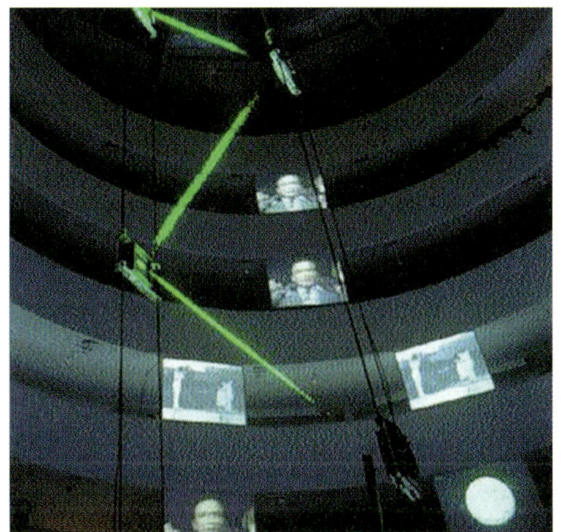

Nam June Païk, Jacob's Ladder, Guggenheim Museum, New York, 2000.

Richard Rogers, Millennium Dome, London, 2000.

TOYO ITO, *TOWER OF WINDS*, YOKOHAMA, 1986

In the Tower of Winds, *Toyo Ito metaphorically represents the visual complexity of Tokyo as a constant and continually changing wind. While the Western city is perceived as a permanent museum of monuments and spaces, Ito considers Tokyo an ephemeral and mutating city, marked not by its buildings but by electrical poles and vending machines, advertising signs and luminous traffic lights. Light here plays both a physical as well as a metaphysical role; the city changes radically after sunset when it reveals its imaginary condition. "Even if the buildings justify their existence during the day, they lose their sense of reality at night." The* Tower of Winds, *with its prosaic presence during the day, its reference to temporary structures, as well as to the spectral nocturnal life, and its constant, shifting spectacle of lights, represents Ito's imaginary city. The Tower – a 21-meter cylinder in front of Yokohama Station – is covered in acrylic mirrors with over a thousand lights bulbs inserted among twelve neon rings with aluminum panels and thirty reflectors at the base. The lights are programmed by a computer to reproduce the various designs that arrive from information gathered from the surrounding environment. At sunset, they transform the tower into a sparkling spectacle of dancing lights and fleeting transparencies. The neon lights run along the length of the tower and the surfaces of the panels appear and disappear, solid or translucent, depending on the reflectors that vary in response to the direction of the wind. The light bulbs, reacting to the surrounding noise, create screens of star dust.*

BILL VIOLA, *THE VEILING*, 1995

The artistic language of Bill Viola brings together music, sound, visual proportions and almost an architecture of images around the essential support of electronics. In this sound-video installation, the images play of a man and woman who move through nocturnal landscapes in a game of lights and shadows that is the effect of the projection of the images on different parallel levels of translucent cloth.

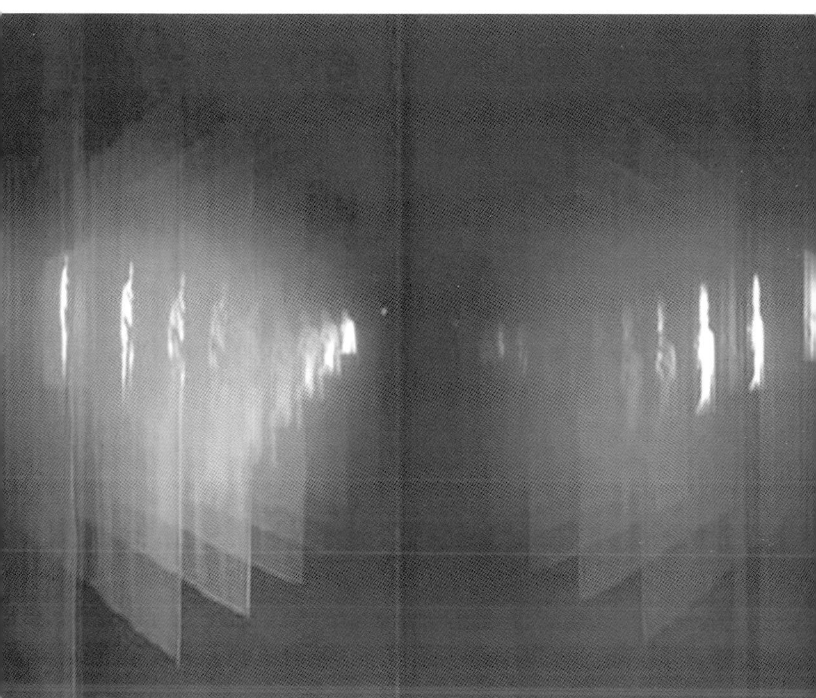

California artist James Turrell uses light as a single instrument in his art to create light volumes, impalpable entities to "probe space". On the heels of his Projections, in which light created three dimensional surfaces within an empty space, in 1991 Turrell created Heavy Water, a dream conceived in 1976 and shared between 1991 and 1992 by ten thousand visitors who immersed themselves in a 24 square meter space that during the day opened up onto the celestial infinite and at night onto the galaxy.

James Turrell, Heavy Water, *image of the interior, 1991.*

Yann Kersalé uses illumination as a support for architecture, which causes this to change from an illuminated body to an illuminating body, a reference point for urban space. The permanent light installation in the port area of Saint-Nazaire, inspired by the analysis of maritime traffic and human flows, seems to reaffirm the presence of the sea and port to its inhabitants. The principle of balisage respects the colors used at the entrance to the port: red at port, green at starboard. Dynamic lights during the night restore the movements of the movable bridges and the shifting crane. Static lights emphasize the forms and materials of the buildings.

GIANNI RANAULO, *VIRTUAL BRIDGE*

This project originated from the concept of the "glocal village" extended to monuments, a use of the virtual on existing monuments, in order to give information and create spectacularizations through a mise en lumière. *Video images are projected onto screens of mist – nebulized water pumped from the Seine and sprayed at high pressure – to create a highly spectacular, almost holographic effect. Light Architecture in this case renews the environment and transfigures this classic monument through the superimposition of light elements, such as water and light, creating, more than any conservative restoration, a reactivation of the monotony of the river's course.*

Beginning with the Pont Neuf in Paris, a visual and virtual interconnection is created among the bridges of the principal European cities thanks to a system of webcams that create a visual link. We have already said that Light Architecture contains an element of interaction with the individual citizen. In this case, Light Architecture takes its strength from the urban context that distinguishes it. In the specific case of the Pont Neuf (where the project involves the still unrestored section of the bridge that faces the Rive Droite), we could speak of an application of modernity to reclaim the identity of the monument.

GIANNI RANAULO, *TOUR MONTPARNASSE*, PARIS, 1996

This design involves a Light Architecture project on the Tour Montparnasse. More than 200 meters high, built during the 1970s as a modern symbol of twentieth century Paris, it has today become a foreign body on the cityscape. The project consists in creating magic virtual rings of artificial fog – 200 meters in diameter, 8 meters high and 60 centimeters thick – obtained through a process of nebulizing water. The rings, on which are projected advertising and multimedia images – including ones via the Internet, with the possibility of receiving and sending messages in real time all over the world – light up consecutively, creating an ascending effect and thus reintroducing the tower with its new image of a multimedia lighthouse in the Paris of the third millennium.

Gianni Ranaulo, *Virtual Towers*, Towers over the Gulf of Naples

Inspired by the Saracen towers that were used not only as defence and watchtowers but above all for communication, this design creates a new element of information and communication through water (if during wartime the towers communicated with fire, today in times of peace they communicate with water): a series of very thin towers, around 120 meters high, built of carbon fiber, almost invisible during the day, materialize in the evening, pumping water directly from the sea and creating – starting from the carbon fiber structure – immaterial rings on which are projected informative, cultural and advertising images. The natural space becomes transfigured, giving life and a new image of the gulf.

3.2 Movement

Movement – an aspect that architects tend to underestimate – helps transfigure a space and render it dynamic. Just as objects are transformed in relation to movement (consider the design of cars, seats, chairs and other furnishings used daily), in the same way habitation should evolve in the same direction. In a society in which physical and mechanical flows take on continually more importance, it is fundamental to consider a "metamorphic" architecture made up of dynamic spaces, in movement, spaces that manage the flows of circulation, the great masses, spaces that evolve over the course of the day, in harmony with the different moments experienced by the city from day to night.

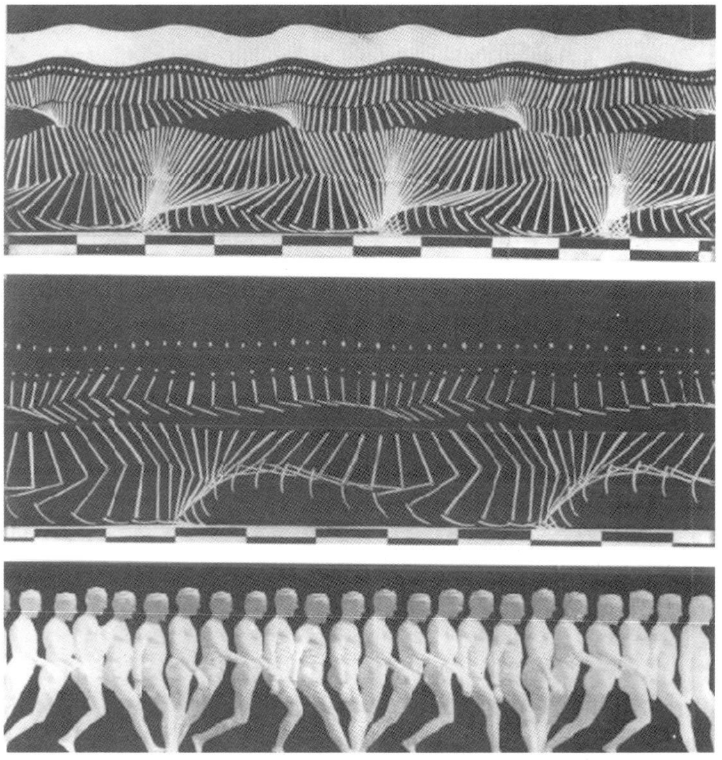

Etienne-Jules Marey, Chrono-photographic study of human locomotion, *1886.*

3.2.1 Conceptual Movement

These are projects that have as their primary characteristic a conceptual-type movement, produced by the visual sensation of the perception of change in an architectural structure as an effect of its own subjective shifts in space. A great example here is definitely represented by the Guggenheim Museum in Bilbao by Frank O. Gehry, in which the dynamic of the spirals and geometric compositions visualizes a rotation and movement.

> Only Gehry fully understands the futurist word "trajectory". In Boccioni as in Gehry, the lines stretched into space may be rectilinear but, in their tension to cleave the air, they are deformed. The straight line becomes an arc, a parabola, indeed a trajectory. (Saggio 97)

Umberto Boccioni, Sviluppo di una bottiglia nello spazio, *1912.*

Umberto Boccioni, Elasticità, *1912.*

Frank O. Gehry, Fred & Ginger, *Prague, 1994.*

Gianni Ranaulo, Galleria del Tritone, Rome, 1995

The plan for the Galleria del Tritone includes the creation of an ecological passageway: the idea is to install, in the center of the tunnel and along its entire 360 meter length, two large screens of vertically falling water, at a distance of around three meters from each other, in order to create a hallway in the inter-space, a magic and symbolic pedestrian space. Conceived as an anti-pollution barrier, using the principle of purification with moisture, the two screens of water become the virtual support for the projection of different types of video images (information that is commercial, institutional, cultural, etc.), thus animating the entire path.

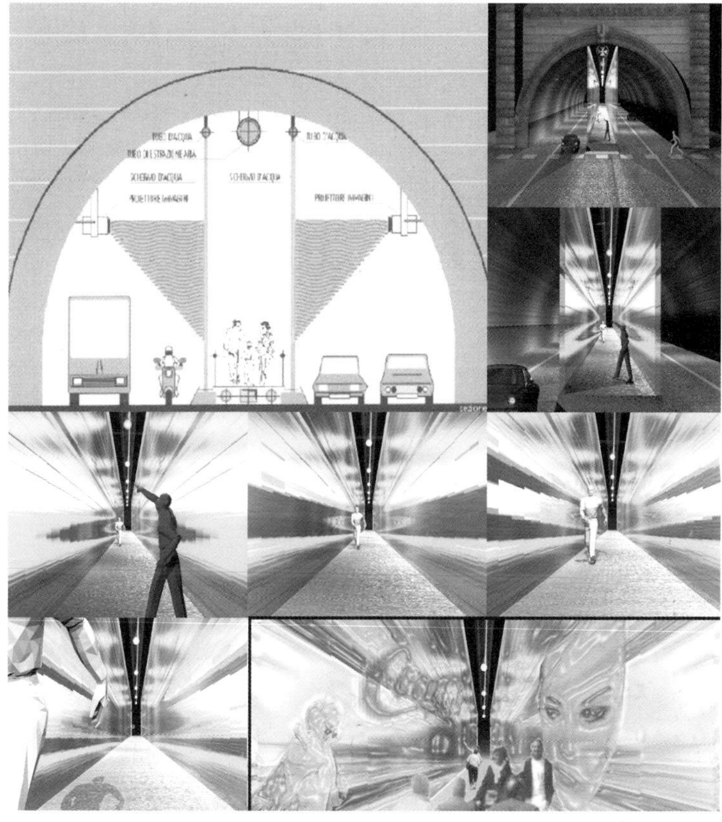

Gianni Ranaulo, Port of Lorient, 1998

This design calls for a project in the area of the Port of Lorient that renews the site while keeping its past intact and at the same time encouraging the development of the city toward more intense tourist and port activities. The large blocks of reinforced concrete that characterize the site are used as a starting point. The idea was to recreate a great metal shell, a kilometer in length and a hundred meters in height, that would cover the entire site, giving access to the great hangars under the roof, in order to create open spaces, with hanging gardens and entertainment areas. This cover has openings which create a continuity of volumes, a continuity of movement and its form, creating a proportion between empty and full spaces. The design of the metal shell gives form to the idea of the movement of the sea and recalls the shape of a submarine.

GIANNI RANAULO, *DREAM TOWER*, NEW YORK

This project is an example of virtual deconstructivism, obtained thanks to the optical effect produced by a glass panel (given a special patent) on which pointed projections of images give the visualization of different depths of field up to around five meters. The glass, only five centimeters thick, has a great range of applications. It can be utilized on different surfaces, even as a double skin, set a small space from the existing facade. This system is ideal for restructuring buildings where the renewal of the image is just as important as structural renovation. At the same time, it gives the construction movement in that its image changes depending on the point of view. So the perspective varies as an effect both of light and movement.

NOX (Lars Spuybroek, Kas Oosterhuis), *Blow Out and Beachness*, 1994-97

These are two "liquid architecture" projects, an invention of Lars Spuybroek of the NOX Architects that derives from a general trend toward studies of the body and genre, in a vision of architecture as prosthesis. Blow Out *is a*

NOX, Blow Out, *Neeltje Jans, Holland.*

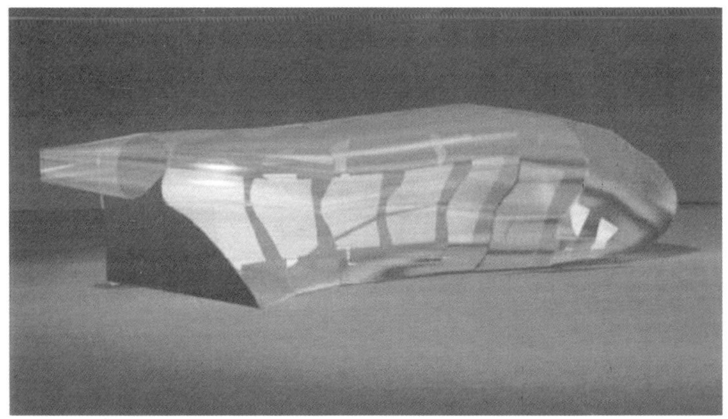

NOX, Blow Out, *Neeltje Jans, Holland.*

design for a block of public bathroom facilities. The finished structure, built around a sequence of steel plates to form a metallic infrastructure covered with cement, develops with a geometrical shape based on an initial curvilinear form. Beachness, the design for a seaside hotel, is based on light, modifiable, fluid architectural structures. Erasing the confines between the beach and parking lot and recreating a single site made up of sand and asphalt where cars act like pedestrians, the design offers a new environmental ecology in which the body and prosthesis are closely connected together in the action. For NOX, the computer was the key to understanding the characteristics of the body and architecture; the body and constructed objects form a new set of topological and geographical relationships.

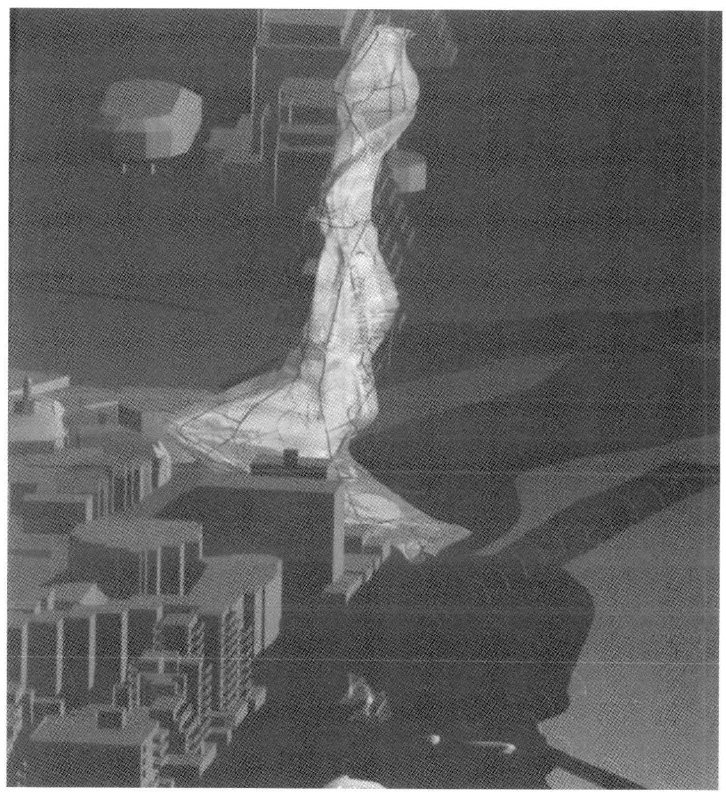

NOX, Beachness, Noordwijk, Holland.

3.2.2 Digital Movement

Peter Eisenmann and Frank O. Gehry are without a doubt a fundamental example of the use of a new digital language in which the computer becomes the materialization of the thought, with the possibility of experimenting with and realizing new forms and applications. In addition, in the past few years a new use has been noted of computers by a new generation of architects – Greg Lynn, Asymptote, Zaha Hadid and others – who push their research toward new frontiers. In particular, the following examples show an architecture in movement, arrived at through the digital, in which spaces and forms are modified.

Frank O. Gehry, Guggenheim Museum, Bilbao, 1997: The structure of the museum was realized with the use of sophisticated technology both in the design phase as well as during construction. "Catia" software, originally used in the aerospace industry, permitted the creation of titanium panels that would have otherwise been impossible with the use of traditional instruments.

PETER EISENMAN, *VIRTUAL HOUSE*

In his work on the virtual house, Eisenman develops a design in which the forms counter one another and find concrete spatiality in movement. The house, generated between two parallel planes, can go above or below the line of the earth; the land is no longer a plate on which to set the volume of the house but becomes a compact fabric that forms the house itself; new spaces open and close one inside the other, defining new possibilities in habitation; light penetrates between the folds of the skin and in the points where the membrane is divided; in an architecture without gravity, the upper part of the house is accessed by sliding inside.

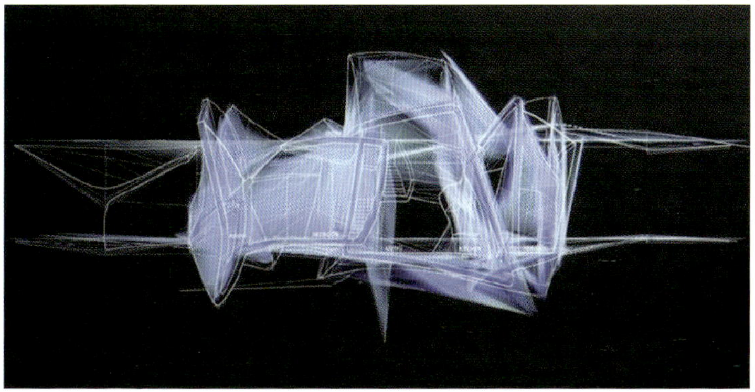

GREG LYNN, *ELECTRA 96*, OSLO, 1996

Utilizing 3D printing technology, Lynn created small scale models, filled with precise details. The starting point was the 5 "nodes" suspended in the Keyhole Gallery of the Oslo Museum, their orbital trajectories coming together to form two groups of composite surfaces. The orbital spaces are supported by aluminum bars on which are fastened circular shaped steel elements, using a series of very light steel struts welded to the structure to give it stability. The entire installation was built of flexible plastic and poly-carbonate leaves that lend an aura of translucence to the entire installation and the space utilized.

Asymptote, New York Stock Exchange (NYSE)

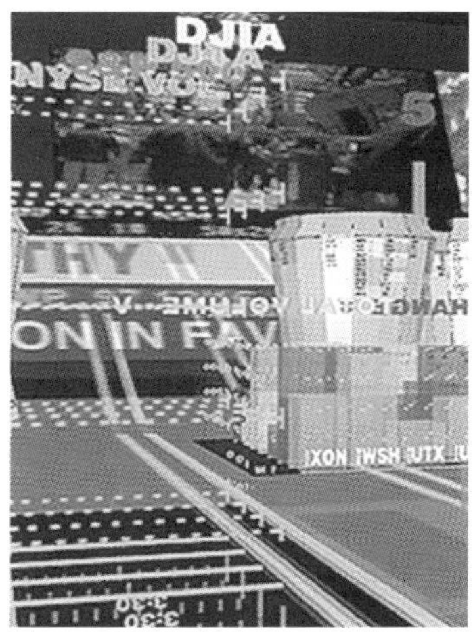

The Asymptote was the first virtual 3D model of the NYSE trading floor. The model, computer generated and projected onto a large video screen, can be navigated and offers information updated in real time. Utilizing advanced technology – such a ultra-flat plasma monitors and "the ramp", a large wall of undulating, blue, luminescent glass that holds up to around 60 monitors – this virtual model is presently used to test the reliability of the technologies that manage daily the commercial and business systems of the NYSE.

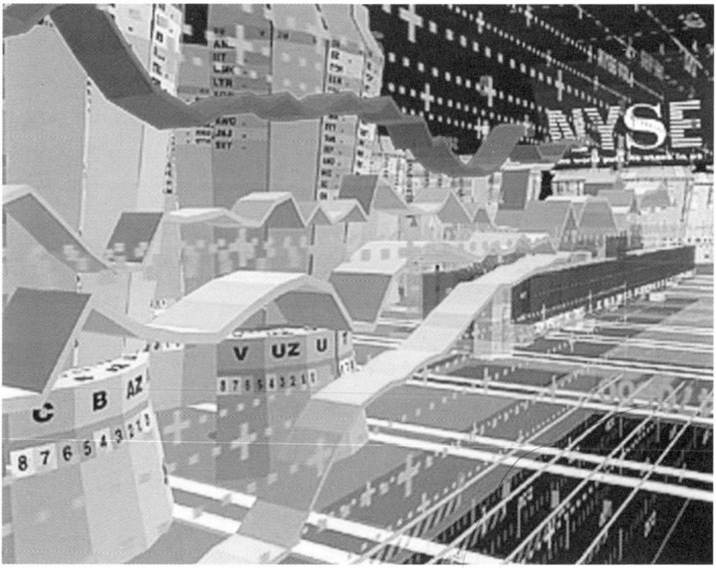

Asymptote, New York Stock Exchange (NYSE).

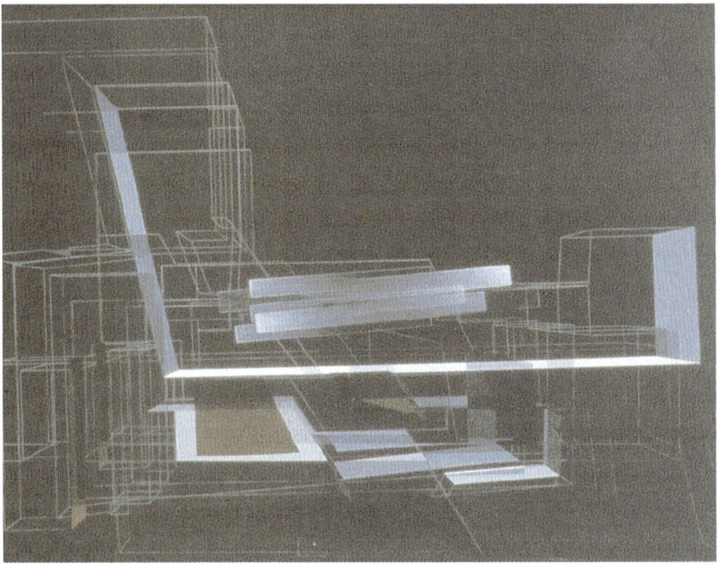

Zaha Hadid, Contemporary Arts Center, Cincinnati, 1999.

3.2.3 EFFECTIVE MOVEMENT

Research into movement in architecture is still ongoing and regards changes in line with the needs of human beings, both in habitations and senses. Included in this category are those examples where architecture actually changes shape depending on space and time, where movement is a necessary function that changes the configuration of the architecture, frequently through a metamorphosis of the space.

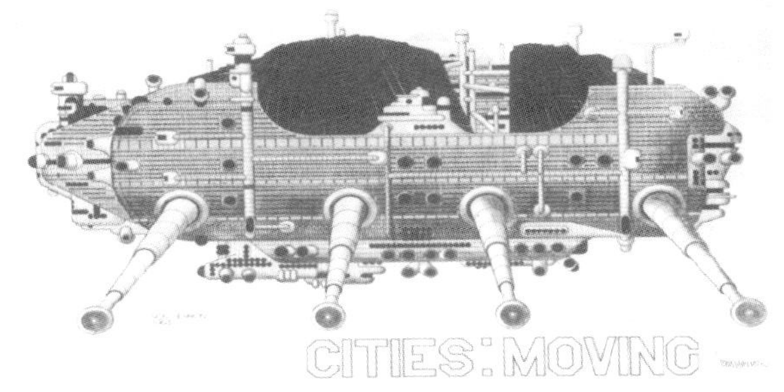

Above: Ron Herron, Cities: Moving, Frankfort-sur-le-Main, *1964. Below: Giacomo Balla,* Velocità d'automobile + luce, *1913.*

Gianni Ranaulo, *Light Breath*, Geneva, 1996

This design, presented at the international competition for ideas for the university building "Unidufour", foresees a large glass veil, made mobile by a combined system of photoelectric cells and pantograph-type mechanical arms, that wraps around the existing building lengthwise thus giving it a new modern and dynamic image. The glass is a patented transparent photovoltaic panel (Graetzler Cell-type for photovoltaic energy using colored, nano-crystalline film) mounted in small square modules (50 x 50 cm). In line with contemporary ecological imperatives, the design transforms the building into a sort of energy sponge, a living skin of glass that breathes with an irregular rhythm in function to the refraction of light rays, thus optimizing absorption. Therefore, the idea is presented as a prototype of an intelligent and ecological way to modernize already existing types of architecture that also includes the projection of various images and information on the undulating facade.

GIANNI RANAULO, GREENPORT, NEW YORK, 1996

This design, presented at the competition for the Greenport Waterfront Park, calls for the creation of a large urban space, ordered and organized by a system of strips running north-south, following the orthogonal arrangement of the original plan of the old city. These strips follow the orientation of the docks of the future tourist port of the village of Greenport, a promenade that connects the sea and city, creating spaces with different functions. The basis of the entire project is flexibility: the module, a five meter wide strip, becomes the guiding element in defining the different spaces in the urban composition: gardens, promenades, scenic walkways, squares, etc. All these strips are orthogonally intersected by the Harborwalk, the scenic walk along the port and sea, elevated four meters above sea level to protect it from the risk of high tides. Starting from the Harborwalk, a series of garden-strips are hinged on the panoramic axis and set on pontoons toward the sea, thus transforming the landscape of the port in line with the tides. This way, the project distributes the various volumes over the water (harbor offices, museum, sports center), along the wharves and within the site outlined by the system of parallel strips.

Gianni Ranaulo, *Piazza della Libertà*, Brest

This design originated from the idea of a dialogue between the functional dimension and the symbolic dimension of a public space in the city center. It is a project based on metamorphosis: the metamorphosis of the city through its history; through the seasons and the presence of the sea inside it; through its daily activities; through the passage from day to night. Public spaces were the starting point, congenial during the day yet inaccessible at night. The solution was the creation of a double square, a "doppia piazza": 1) a "piazza-sagrato", "town square-churchyard", shaped like a seagull's wing (a reference to the poetry of Jacques Prevert and the image of the Atlantic Ocean) that at night is transformed into a fountain-waterfall; 2) a covered square under the seagull's wing that at night is transformed into a magical pool of water, surrounded by spaces for expositions, shops, boutiques, bars, restaurants and services, that animate this underlying perspective, made accessible by broad steps on the upper urban level. The movement of the large plate of the "piazza-sagrato" is executed by a system of hydraulic pistons, placed at the two longitudinal extremities, that cause the entire urban plane to oscillate around a central axis.

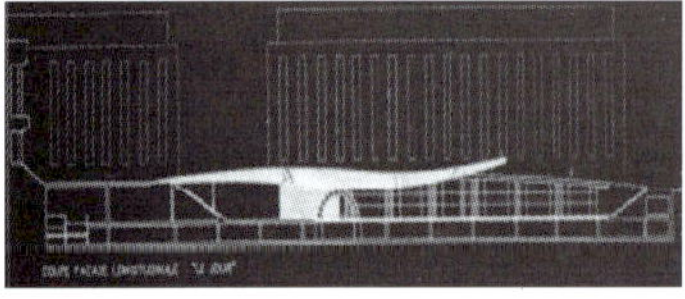
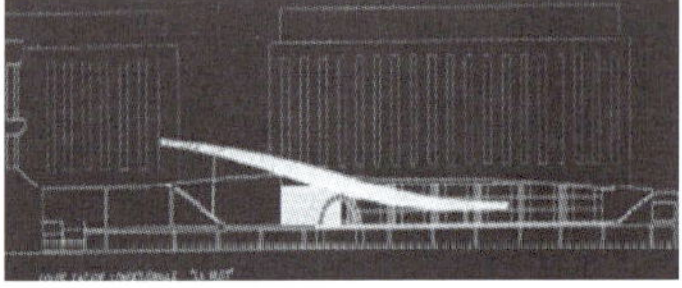

The design by Watanabe for the National Diet Building plans for the construction of a building with no specific form, made of flexible joints, capable of tightening or loosening to modify the form of the building. The exterior of the building is covered in an elastic material divided into small cells (composed of photosynthetic and chromatospheric elements activated by solar energy), joined together almost as if to represent the skin of a living organism. The external facade is also a large screen on which images of the interior activities are projected. The overall form of the building is determined by two factors: one whereby the form reflects the activities carried out inside the structure (it expands when the Diet is in session and contracts when it is in recess; it expands when there are many visitors and contracts when the building is empty); the other whereby the form of the building is determined by external forces (not only wind, earthquakes and atmospheric agents but also public opinion and the media). Essentially, the Diet Building behaves like a living thing, capable of assuming different forms depending on the circumstances.

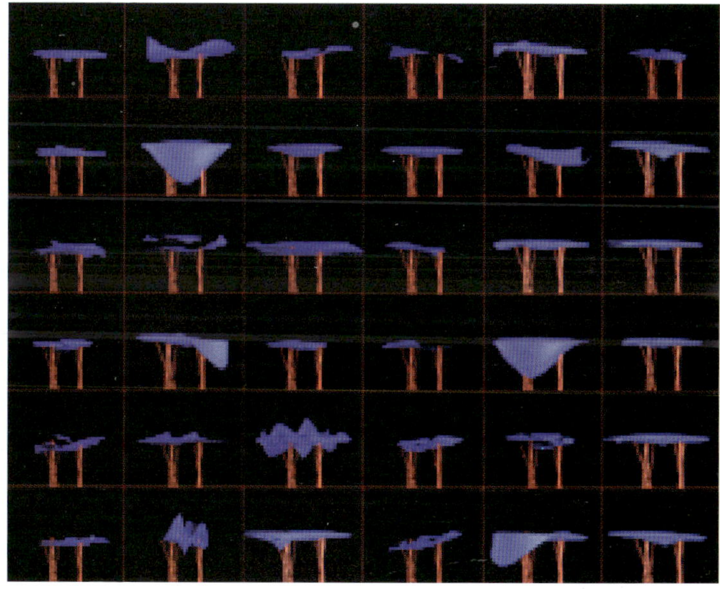

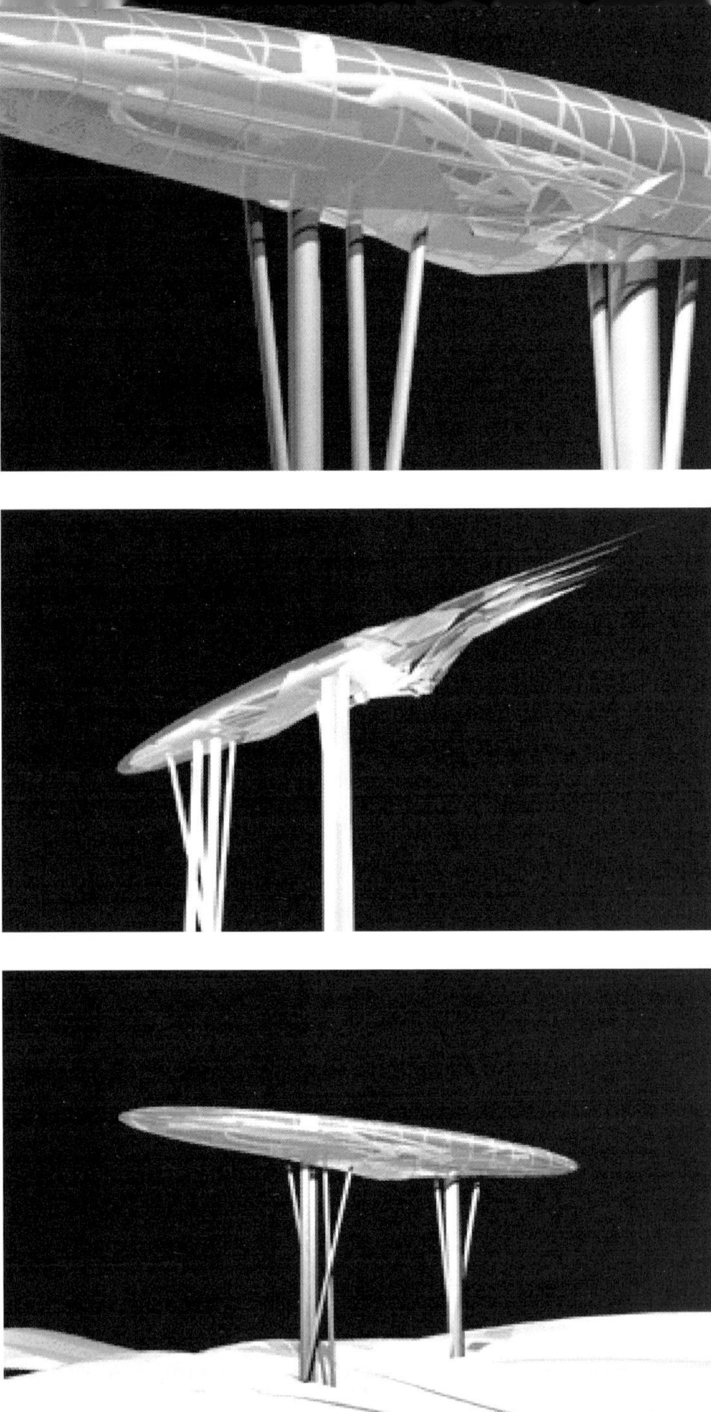

3.3 Information

To the three geometrical dimensions that not long ago determined the perception of the relief of real space, now a third dimension of matter is added: after "mass" and "energy", the dimension of "information" makes its entrance into the history of reality [...]. Following the material and geometric volume of an object is the immaterial and electronic one of information. [...] Just as the European Renaissance would be unimaginable without the invention of the perspective of real space, so geopolitical globalization will be inseparable from the unification of this perspective of real time and this new spatial-temporal RELIEF coming from the electromagnetic irradiation of telecommunications. (Virilio 2000)

3.3.1 MEDIA BUILDING

Light Architecture, applied to the individual building, creates the Media Building®: the interactive multimedia facade.

Jenny Holzer, Installation View, *Guggenheim Museum, New York, 1990.*

Jenny Holzer, Survival Series, *installation on Yonge Street, Toronto, 1986.*

This application of architecture, on buildings either already existing or to be constructed, makes up a new network system; the Media Building is, in effect, a new tool of communication and information that can be: 1. institutional (publicly useful information, public meetings, communication between cities); 2. cultural (events, news, etc.); 3. advertising (company, local, national); 4. social (public service advertising); 5. personal (Internet, SMS, long-distance communication).

This is a patented system, created thanks to the retro-projection of images onto various transparent supports: glass with angular vision, iridescent points, iridescent micro-opalization, or treated marble-glass. The use of high-definition projectors – connected in

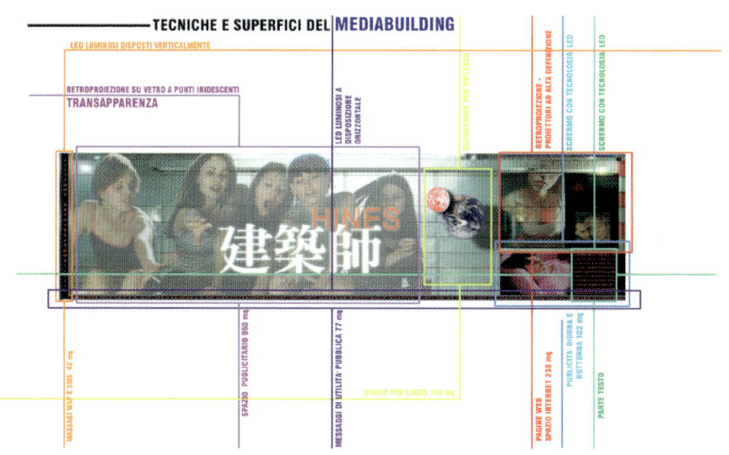

series and run by a computer – helps create images in a large format, thanks to the multi-branch system, and gives the effect of the appearance of images on transparency (trans-appearance). The glass therefore represents the border between the real world and the virtual one, their fusion performed in the Media Building itself: the real image behind the glass melds into that of the projection on the first level (stereo-reality).

In a favorable moment of significant growth in the billboard and poster market (+ 8% in the last year, with a percentage of billboard/posters in overall advertising investments of 3.1%), the

Media Building – designed as such – would expand the range of media available for outdoor advertising: small sizes, dynamic images, high definition, sophisticated technology, three dimensional effects, interactivity, large modularity and the possibility of modifying the advertising based on the time of day and therefore the target audience.
From the strictly architectural point of view, the Media Building could be an important element in renewing the urban landscape (going beyond the present limits of those silk-screened surfaces on facades built up till now). There are many different potential methods of application, with particular attention to areas of the city that have fallen into disuse, the "black holes of the city", buildings from the 1960s that have compromised the image of our cities, even arriving in historic city centers.

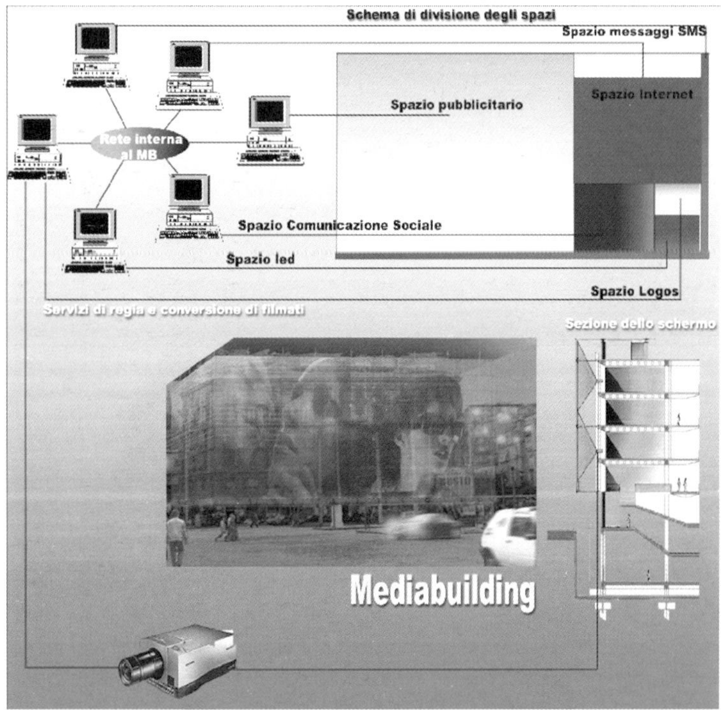

PIANO, ROGERS, FRANCHINI, CENTRE POMPIDOU, PARIS, 1971-77

The initial design for the Centre Pompidou, later modified over the course of the six years of construction, is an early example of a multimedia building that houses culture and gives information:. "It would have been the largest television screen in France, without having any production structure behind it", confirmed Renzo Piano in a 1993 interview. In fact, the project planned for, among other innovations, a large LED screen on the main facade that would have allowed the reception of information related to events at the Center or current cultural and political news. Despite the changes with respect to the original project, the Centre Pompidou still remains an early and prime example of a light, flexible and multimedia structure.

VENTURI, SCOTT BROWN & ASSOCIATES, WHITEHALL FERRY TERMINAL, NEW YORK, 1996

The Staten Island Ferry terminal, added to the skyline of New York, from which it is differentiated because of its slightly curvilinear form, is seen as the architectural and symbolic entrance to the city. The great, innovative video screen, on the southern side facing the water, makes up the urban face of the terminal: a large, electronic notice board in the shape of a flag on which electronic images are projected (designs, information and news, sports events); the predominant iconic image is the fragment of the flag, also visible from the side opposite the bay.

GIANNI RANAULO, EGINARDO BUILDING, MILANO

Day.

Night.

Virtual.

The Eginardo Building has an architecture like many buildings in Milan, weakened by time, but capable of conserving those characteristics from which a new vital fluid could give birth to a new creature. The design consists of a Media Building with a double ventilated skin superimposed on the existing facade and a transformation of the facade facing the parking lot into a terrace and winter garden. The double glass facade, bringing together comfort and transparency, gives dignity and elegance to the whole structure and supplies the offices inside with a pleasant, temperate micro-climate. The skin, of specially patented, angular-vision glass, allows perfect visibility from the inside toward the outside, while, seen from the exterior of the building, the translucent effect created by iridescent micro-points allows the evening retro-projection of images and advertising information, even on-line. The new facade thus becomes a chance for urban communication and the structure of the screen precisely modulates light, transparency, reflections and projections of images, reacting in a different way depending on the time of day or night.

Gianni Ranaulo, *4D Down Town*, Milan, 2001

This project attempts to render the building completely open along the axes of via Bergognona and via Tortona, creating a "piazza", and at the same time responding to the needs for flexibility in functional spaces. The opening of the ground floor toward the piazza is arranged with a system of stairs, ramps and terraces. The flow of people works to animate the open gallery. The project is characterized by two large roofs: one translucent that creates the covered piazza and the other trans-apparent with projections of images that are superimposed on the sky. The spectacularization of the flows (physical) of people melds in with that of the flows (immaterial) of information. The piazza, defined by three symbolic axes (X, Y, Z) thus becomes a gigantic multimedia, interactive screen that gives center stage to the cultural, informative and commercial activities of the neighborhood and city.

FOX & FOWLE, FOUR TIMES SQUARE, NEW YORK

The design for the skyscraper at Four Times Square, where the technology stock market, NASDAQ, is headquartered, is an example of the application of new technologies on a grand scale in a place where business and entertainment come together. Despite this fact, this skyscraper is not yet an actual Media Building but a building in transition since the technology utilized is still too expensive and sophisticated (18,677,760 LEDs, each supplied with its own individual electric feed) and the design is definitely invasive during the day.

Renzo Piano, KPN Telecom, Rotterdam, 2000

Inaugurated last September, this building is a tower with a facade-screen utilized for presenting works of art and communication between the local administration and citizens. The images do not cover the entire facade but only its structural elements and serve to integrate the media information and the architecture of contemporary Rotterdam. The tower – situated at the same height as the old terminal via a two floor platform on which it rests – is visually connected to the bridge and square and helps organize the surrounding area, giving continuity and coherence to the urban space.

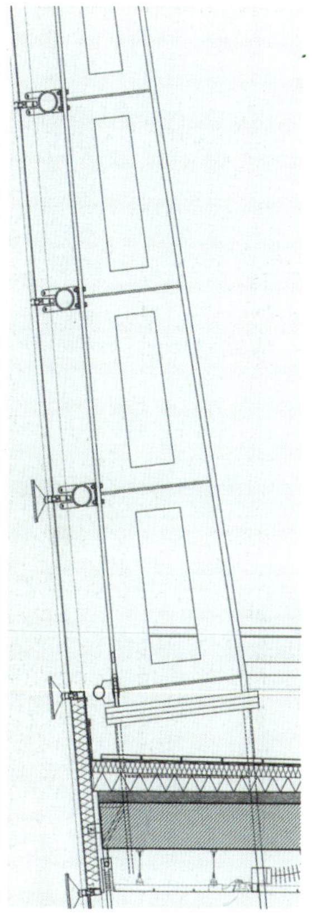

Jean Nouvel, Andel Building, Prague

The Andel Building, in the Schmikov section of Prague, faces onto a metro station where more than twenty million passengers come through every day. The design includes four buildings, connected by passageways, with a large common roof garden at the top. The special aspect of this project is the treatment of the facade on the street. Under the white and gray cement pattern of the windows and the large glass section of the upper floors, there is the silk-screen of a series of images: a poem by Jan Palach, a group of clouds and a gigantic photo of an angel on the semi-circular section that terminates the building. On the street level, under the shops, a series of oblique marquees with advertising billboards enlivens the city and shows off the function of the construction.

This hotel, created by Nouvel in Lucerne, is a tribute to the cinema. Images from some of the greatest films in the history of film-making are projected onto the ceiling of each room, images that, through a play of reflection and transparency in the materials used, can also be seen publicly by passers-by, transforming the hotel by night into a complex tableau vivant featuring the characters from the films. Each room is furnished in relation to the film and there is a spatial cross-reference between the different levels, like the glass partition that creates a visual communication between the hall and the restaurant.

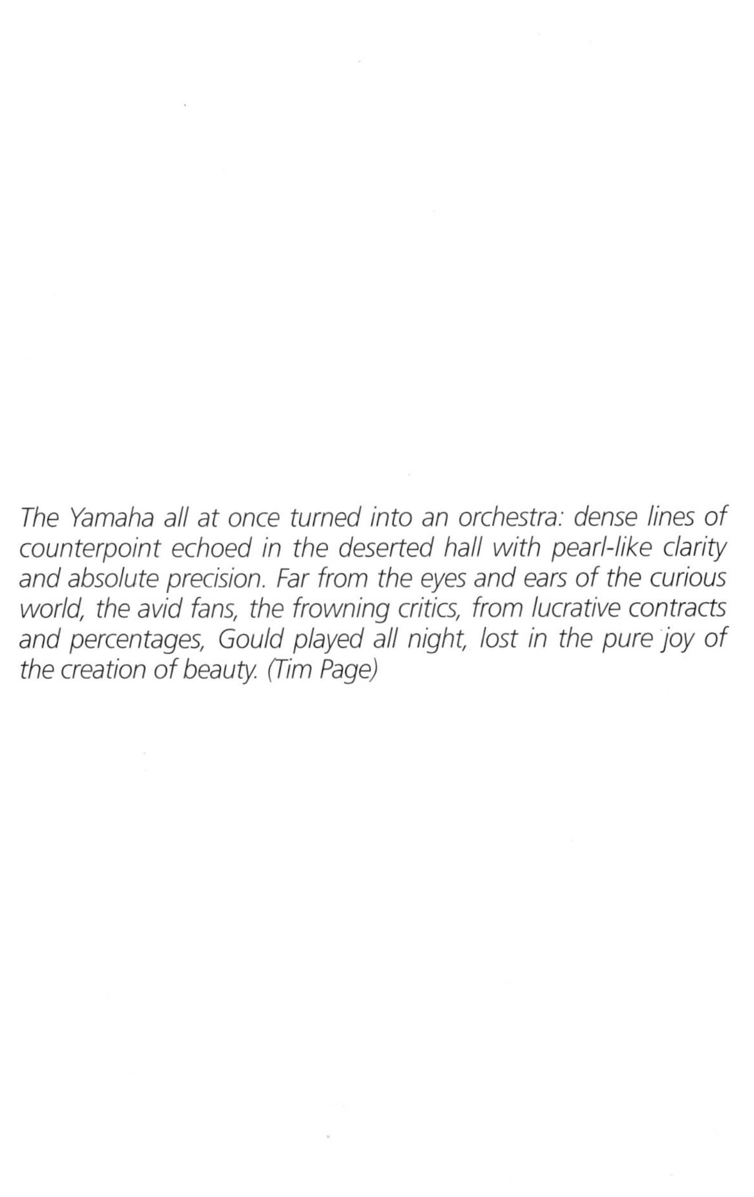

The Yamaha all at once turned into an orchestra: dense lines of counterpoint echoed in the deserted hall with pearl-like clarity and absolute precision. Far from the eyes and ears of the curious world, the avid fans, the frowning critics, from lucrative contracts and percentages, Gould played all night, lost in the pure joy of the creation of beauty. (Tim Page)

Future is Light

Afterword by Carlo Massarini

Science Fiction had already foreseen everything. Or almost everything. Voyages to the moon, voyages even further, guided by an intelligent, in fact human, computer. Microscopic dimensions of men and technologies. Voyages to other planets where other species rule. Bionic men, androids, replicants. Robots that live two hundred years before choosing human mortality. Cyborgs that travel through time. Science Fiction had above all imagined voyages outside ourselves.

Then, as a legacy of the Cold War, a network arrived called Arpanet and that strange, dark form of Science Fiction appeared called Cyberpunk: not space but cyberspace. Not far away but here, simultaneously in two parallel realities. A fifth dimension, with its virtuality, interactivity, globality. With its immaterial architecture and its lightness, much more sustainable than our daily life, weighted down by atoms, gravity, bureaucracy. No one imagined it, no one foresaw it. But the Net has arrived and has changed the world. The world of information, communication, relationships. And, though nothing will ever be the same again, we need no longer consider how to adapt things, how to do better that which has already been done before. It is useless to attempt to replicate a well known model. If the paradigm changes, the scenario changes. We are in another movie.

It is objectively difficult to imagine our future. The Internet is a recent invention and the generation who invented it may not finally be the generation who really understands what can be done with it. Sure, now we think that within ten or twenty years we will all potentially be connected, individual receiving-transmitting nodes that pulse in a ubiquitous Net, invisible, natural, like the air we breathe.

Once again, the difficult thing is not to imagine the technology: basically, the only limit to inventions is our own fantasy, history shows that. The difficult thing is to understand whether or not, and if so how, it will change mankind, as individuals and a group. Because mankind changes slower than technology. The year 2000 was once imagined as something like *Metropolis*, and here we

are: cars do not fly, and mankind is still, for the most part, firmly on the earth. However, in the meantime, technology has transformed immobile communications to mobile. Even financial flows, intellectual property, the distribution of goods and information, all have become mobile, freed from the material. Light.
Will technology also transform architecture, in other words that immobile communication that has characterized history? Even though architecture has, to a great extent, lost it profound power of communication, pyramids, temples, royal palaces, dolmen, skyscrapers, towers are all there to remind us that buildings can speak. They tell a story. At times esoteric, at times obvious, but always connected to the culture and nature of an area. Will we return to the future, to an architecture that goes back to being communication; a mobile communication that goes beyond the esthetic and material, beyond cultural, spatial and temporal barriers?
Light Architecture is a leap in this direction. Well beyond structural lightness, the esthetics of transparency, the concept behind media buildings is that of a terminal. Even better, a node in a network, capable of being autonomous, but also integrated into a more complex system. Just like the Web, the Media Building is interactive, global, light. The Internet has gone from the desktop PC, seated, to the mobile phone, standing. With the MB, the Internet leaves the house and enters the city. It leaves the private and becomes public.
The MB is one of those projects that are the beginning of something that it is not easy to define, at least at present. We have all seen the truncated pyramids in *Blade Runner* where a Japanese woman winks at the city. We have walked underneath the round NASDAQ tower where the futures of capital, technological innovation and information all meet. Among the photos in this book, you have seen many windows open onto the future. So, imagine all these buildings no longer as isolated totems but nodes in a network. One that speaks, that shows, that warns, that remembers, that informs, that helps.
Perhaps the future of communication will also pass by here.

Bibliographical Notes

ESSENTIAL REFERENCES
Baudrillard 97 – Jean Baudrillard, *Illusion, désillusion esthétiques*, Sens & Tonka éditeurs, Paris 1997.
Calvino 88 – Italo Calvino, *Lezioni americane*, Garzanti, Milan 1988.
Cités 87 – *Cités-Cinés*, Éditions Ramsay, La Villette, Paris 1987.
Galofaro 99 – Luca Galofaro, *Digital Eisenman*, Birkhäuser, Basel - Boston - Berlin 2000.
Hulten 86 – Pontus Hultén, *Futurismo & Futurismi*, Bompiani, Milan 1986.
Johansen 95 – John Johansen, *A Life in the Continuum of Architecture*, L'Arca Edizioni, Milan 1995.
Le Corbusier 75 – *Le Corbusier. Quando le cattedrali erano bianche*, Faenza editrice, 1975.
Nouvel 94 – *Jean Nouvel, El Croquis*, no. 65-66, 1994.
Riley 95 – Terence Riley, *Light Construction*, The Museum of Modern Art, New York 1995.
Saggio 97 - Antonino Saggio, *Frank O. Gehry*, Testo & Immagine, Turin 1997.
Virilio 2000 – Paul Virilio, *La bomba informatica*, Raffaello Cortina Editore, Milan 2000.

OTHER REFERENCES
Agence des Gares-AREP: Parcours 1988-1998, Edizioni Diagonale, Rome 1998.
Jacob Baal-Teshuva, *Christo & Jeanne-Claude*, Taschen, Köln 1995.
Marie-France Boyer, *Le génie des cabanes*, Thames & Hudson, London 1993.
Casabella, no. 658, July-August 1998.
Crossing, no. 1, Media Building, December 2000.
Domus, no. 831, November 2000.
Habitat, Technology & Architectural Envelopes, Permasteelisa, 1999.
Images et imaginaires d'architecture, Centre George Pompidou, Paris 1984.
Yann Kersalé, *Expéditions Lumière*, Galeries Enrico Navarra-Jousse Seguin, Paris 1994.
L'Arca, November 1992, no. 65.
L'Arca International, September 1999, no. 30.
H. Pearman (ed.), *Contemporary World Architecture*, Phaidon, London 1998.
K. Sakamura, H. Suzuki (eds.), *The Virtual Architecture*, Tokyo University Digital Museum, Tokyo 1997.
James Turrell, Beaux-Arts magazine, April 2000.
Wallpaper, September 2000.

Notes on the Images

1. THE ORIGINS
Antonio Sant'Elia: Hulten 1986.
Agence des Gares-AREP: Parcours 1988-1998, Edizioni Diagonale, Rome 1998.
Le Corbusier: Le Corbusier 75.
Doug Aitken: *www.adobe.com*.
Metropolis: Cités 87.
Sarah Morris: *www.petzel.com*.

LOT/EK: *www.LOTEKarchitecture.com*.

2. THE IDEA
Shigeko Kubota: *www.artincontext.org*.
Olafur Eliasson: *www.uol.com.br/bienal*; *www.pascal.alesco.it*.
Erick Van Egeraat Associated: *Habitat, Technology & Architectural Envelopes*, Permasteelisa, 1999.

3. THE PROJECTS
Asymptote: *www.asymptote-architecture.com*.
Santiago Calatrava: H. Pearman (eds.), *Contemporary World Architecture*, Phaidon, London 1998.
Dennis Oppenheim: *www.artincontext.org*.
Sigheru Ban: *L'Arca*, November 1992, no. 65.
John M. Johansen: *A Life in the Continuum of Architecture*, L'Arca Edizioni, Milan 1995.
Toyo Ito: K. Sakamura, H. Suzuki (eds.), *The Virtual Architecture*, Tokyo University Digital Museum, Tokyo 1997.
Jean Nouvel: Nouvel 94.
Christo: Jacob Baal-Teshuva, *Christo & Jeanne-Claude*, Taschen, Köln 1995.
Coop Himmelb(l)au: *http://194.185.28.38/it/expoing2.html*.
Aldo Rossi: H. Pearman, *op. cit.*
Images of sheds: Marie-France Boyer, *Le génie des cabanes*, Thames & Hudson, London 1993.
Dam Graham: *www.diacenter.org*.
Kovac Malone: *Wallpaper*, September 2000.
Yann Kersalé: Yann Kersalé, *Expéditions Lumière*, Galeries Enrico Navarra-Jousse Seguin, Paris 1994.
Norman Foster: H. Pearman, *op. cit.*
Nam June Paik: *www.artincontext.org*.
Richard Rogers: *Ulisse 2000*, February 2001.
James Turrell: *James Turrell, Beaux-Arts magazine*, April 2000.
Etienne-Jules Marey: Hulten 86.
Frank O. Gehry: H. Pearman, *op. cit.*
Umberto Boccioni: Hulten 86.
NOX: *L'Arca International*, September 1999, no. 30.
Frank O. Gehry: *Habitat, Technology & Architectural Envelopes* cit.
Peter Eisenmann: Luca Galofaro, *Digital Eisenman* cit..
Greg Lynn: *www.basilisk.com/mFORM*; *www.glform.com*.
Ron Herron: *Images et imaginaires d'architecture*, Centre George Pompidou, Paris 1984.
Giacomo Balla: Hulten 86.
Makoto Sei Watanabe: *www.makoto-architect.com*.
Jenny Holzer: *www.artincontext.org*; *http://adaweb.walkerart.org*.
Piano-Rogers: H. Pearman, *op. cit.*
Venturi, Scott Brown & Associates: *Casabella*, no. 658, July-August 1998.
Renzo Piano: *Crossing*, no. 1, *Media Building*, December 2000.
Fox & Fowle: *Media Building*, December 2000.
Jean Nouvel: Jean Nouvel, *Les éléments de l'architecture*, Adam Biro, 1999.
Jean Nouvel: *Domus*, no. 831, November 2000.
Gianni Ranaulo: *www.ranaulo.com*.

New Wombs
Electronic Bodies and Architectural Disorders
Maria Luisa Palumbo
ISBN 3-7643-6294-4

New Flatness
Surface Tension in Digital Architecture
Alicia Imperiale
ISBN 3-7643-6295-2

Digital Design
New Frontiers for the Objects
Paolo Martegani / Riccardo Montenegro
ISBN 3-7643-6296-0

The Architecture of Intelligence
Derrick de Kerckhove
ISBN 3-7643-6451-3

Advanced Technologies
Building in the Computer Age
Valerio Travi
ISBN 3-7643-6450-5

Aesthetics of Total Serialism
Contemporary Research from Music to Architecture
Markus Bandur
ISBN 3-7643-6449-1

History of Form* Z
Pierluigi Serraino
ISBN 3-7643-6563-3

Digital Gehry
Bruce Lindsay
ISBN 3-7643-6562-5

For our free catalog please contact:

Birkhäuser – Publishers for Architecture
P. O. Box 133, CH-4010 Basel, Switzerland
Tel. ++41-(0)61-205 07 07; Fax ++41-(0)61-205 07 92
e-mail: sales@birkhauser.ch
http://www.birkhauser.ch